This I Believe

This
I Believe

Lawrence Welk
with Bernice McGeehan

Prentice-Hall, Inc., Englewood Cliffs, New Jersey

Printed in the United States of America

Prentice-Hall International, Inc., London/Prentice-Hall of Australia, Pty. Ltd., Sydney/Prentice-Hall of Canada, Ltd., Toronto/ Prentice-Hall of India Private Ltd., New Delhi/Prentice-Hall of Japan, Inc., Tokyo/ Prentice-Hall of Southeast Asia Pte. Ltd., Singapore/Whitehall Books Limited, Wellington, New Zealand

10 9 8 7 6 5 4 3

Library of Congress Cataloging in Publication Data
Welk, Lawrence.
  This I believe.
  1. Welk, Lawrence, 1904-   I. McGeehan,
Bernice. II. Title.
ML422.W33A29   785.4'1'0924 [B]   79-17541
ISBN 0-13-919092-9

Preface

For the past ten years or so, I have tried to share my deepest feelings with our friends and fans across the nation, through my books. In all of them I've tried to express the tremendous joy and gratitude I feel, at having been fortunate enough to live in this country. I've tried also, to point out the reasons why I believe our orchestra and I have been able to build such truly fulfilled lives.

In *My America, Your America*, I wrote rather extensively of the system we use in our band, and the ways in which I felt it could be used on a more widespread basis to help all of us—particularly, our precious young people. I also tried to describe, as best I could, how powerful our system is in achieving the inner peace and personal fulfillment that, to me, spell real success.

Well, that was three years ago, and in the intervening months, I have come to believe so strongly in the merits of some of the "suggestions" I made in that book, I'm now going to recommend them unreservedly! One or two of my "recommendations" may surprise you a little—may even shock you. But I hope with all my heart that you'll consider them, evaluate them, and then—if you agree with me, help me put them into effect.

I'm going to tell you some stories about the orchestra in this book too, to explain my recommendations and beliefs. In fact, I'm going to tell you so much about the orchestra and how we tape our television show, you may be able to start a band of your own!

I'm going to tell you about our other business enterprises too—The Lawrence Welk Plaza, our restaurant-motel complex in Escondido, and our business office in Santa Monica—to show you how well our system can work in other media.

I'm going to indicate, in dollars-and-cents terms, how well our profit-sharing plan serves our employees, and outline, once again, the Welk Freedom System, which has brought us such unbelievable success and happiness.

Finally, I'm going to share with you the philosophies and moral truths which have guided and supported me all my life.

I'm supposed to be in my "golden" years, now that I'm in my seventies. But, my dear, dear friends—for me, all the years have been golden, even the harsh early ones when I was still on the farm. Even then I had my music. And always, throughout my life, I have been privileged to do the work I love, with the people I love, in the country I love.

Recently, a reporter asked me how I'd like to be remembered.

Well, certainly, music is and always will be, my life. I'm deeply, humbly proud of the place my orchestra and I have been able to create in the hearts of so many people across the nation. It would be very nice to be remembered as a man who brought music to America.

But if I could be remembered as a man who opened a door for young people, as one who helped restore the freedom and opportunity that gave this country birth, and a man who helped reestablish the unshakeable moral principles upon which a life can be truly and nobly built— then I would feel my life had been of real worth.

It is for these reasons I write this book. It is my earnest hope and prayer that some of my thoughts and suggestions will touch you, and together, we in this nation, can begin to live truly fulfilled and truly free lives, once again.

Contents

Dedicated to the young people of America, in the hope that this book will help free them to begin building better, happier, and more completely fulfilled lives for themselves, and the generations yet to come.

I would like to thank Louise Carroll for typing the manuscript not only of this book, but all my books; and for doing so with perfection and total dedication.

Part One

Our Wonderful Young People

1.

Our Audience Is Getting Younger

For many years I was under the impression that our television audience was made up primarily of the "mothers and fathers" of America. And that was fine with me! After all we grew up together, lived through some pretty exciting years together, danced together. All during the thirties and forties the "mamas and papas" listened to our little band, as the boys and I played throughout the Dakotas and Nebraska and Kansas and Iowa and Minnesota. Then in 1951, through the miracle of television, they began listening and dancing to us all over the United States. They even put us back on the air when we were dropped by ABC in 1971, encouraging us to go into syndication, where their loyal friendship has helped us achieve the greatest success of our lifetime. It's no wonder I feel such a special affection and gratitude for them. The mothers and fathers of this land will always have a very high rating with me.

And now in the past few years, they have done something else very wonderful—their children and grandchildren have been coming over to us too! I first began noticing this phenomenon along about 1970 on our concert tours, when I spotted more and more bright young faces popping up in our audiences. Next, the girls in the office began reporting that more fan mail was coming in from younger viewers (some so young they would scrawl just a few words on lined school paper, darling little notes I just loved). I was absolutely delighted at this turn of events, because one of the great joys of my life has been my relationship with young people. Nothing gives me more pleasure than to discover and develop young talent—something you may have suspected from the parade of talented young people who have appeared on our show over the years. Incidentally, I'll let you in on a little secret right now. All those fresh young faces you see on your television screen are there by design. They're young enough to stand extreme camera closeups, and they add a certain freshness, a youthful glow, a "prettiness" to our show. Back where the lights aren't quite so bright sit our excellent musicians—aging a little, perhaps, but still not in the same league with the boss! It's not that they can't stand the closeups. It's just that in the process of becoming the superb professionals they are, a couple of them have developed a wrinkle here, a double chin there, and maybe a bald spot or two. But that doesn't matter. Their musicianship is what counts, and that is so fine, so thorough, that it forms the solid foundation on which we build the entire show. And it's the young ones up front, just starting out on the same path, who add the youthful sparkle that gives our show a certain brightness. And tying the whole thing together is the "father" up front, the one waving the baton—me!

Well, I got off the track a little there. After all, when you get to be seventy-six, your mind tends to

wander a bit (if it remembers to function at all, that is!).
But what I started to say was that there has been a
definite emphasis on youth in the past few years, both
in our show and in our audience. And I've been very,
very happy about it. But I don't think I actually realized
what a big audience of young folks we had, till one fine
spring day in April of 1978, when I met about five
hundred of them in person. The experience was so
overwhelming, I'd like to tell you about it.

2.

Children! You're Spoiling an Old Man

On April 13, 1978, I flew to Dodge City, Kansas, to receive an honorary Doctorate of Humanities degree from St. Mary of the Plains College. (Actually, I flew to Wichita, Kansas, first, partly because my good friend Dwight Wilson lives there, and partly because there is no direct flight from Los Angeles to Dodge City!) Dwight and I had a fine visit for a couple of days, and then his grandson, Jon Williams, drove me to Dodge City for the graduation exercises at the college.

I was very nervous about the whole thing. The extent of my own formal education is four grades at Sts. Peter and Paul parochial school in Strasburg, North Dakota, so I've always felt a little nervous being around learned men. And when Jon and I arrived, and found that the ceremonies were being held in the beautiful church on campus, with thirty priests celebrating the Mass along with Bishop Gerber of the Diocese, I got so rattled I could barely get through my acceptance speech! It seemed almost incredible to me that an

uneducated farm boy, a son of immigrant parents, was
being so highly honored. But, that's America.

Next morning Jon and I drove back to
Wichita. He and his grandpa and I have been friends for
years and years and have a small share together in the oil
business, so on the way home we decided to stop for a
quick look at "our" oil well. On the way I began to get
ravenously hungry. "Jon," I said, "I'm starving! We
haven't had a bite to eat since early this morning."

"Okay," said Jon agreeably. "I'm hungry, too.
There's a nice little town coming up soon—Macksville.
We can stop there."

Presently, a cluster of buildings loomed up on
the highway, and Jon pulled to a stop in front of one of
them, Pinkie's Cafe, a spanking clean little place decorated with cute toy trains running around the plate rails.
The room was almost empty when we walked in, but
within minutes it began to fill up. People seemed to
spring out of the walls, all of them smiling and welcom-
ing us. We chatted with two pretty young school girls in
their mid-teens, who asked for an autograph and then
prevailed on me to write them an excuse so the principal
would know they weren't kidding when they told him
they were late because they'd been talking to Lawrence
Welk. "He'll never believe *that*!" they said. "Okay," I
laughed, "maybe this will help." I scrawled a few words
on one of my business cards and gave it to them.

Next thing I knew, a man came bursting
through the door, rushed up, took a close look at me,
and then introduced himself as Jerry Paden, the principal of the school. He urged me to come over and say
hello to the children.

"Please do, Mr. Welk," he said. "It would
mean so very much to them."

"Well—how long would it take you to get them all together?" I inquired.

"Two minutes." he said promptly. "One!"

"Okay," I laughed, "Jon and I will be over as soon as we finish breakfast."

"Wonderful," he cried, racing out the door, "wonderful!"

Jon and I finished our nice breakfast, then walked across the street to the school—a handsome building housing all the grades, kindergarten through high school—and into the biggest surprise of my life. Not expecting a thing, I walked into the school gymnasium and straight into the greatest longest loudest warmest most overwhelming ovation of my lifetime! I just couldn't believe it. I stood rooted to the spot (I don't know for sure, but I have a hunch my jaw was dropping) while that tremendous applause rolled and swirled and thundered all around me. One minute, two minutes—five minutes! Never in my life have I received a welcome like that one. Everybody was smiling and everybody was applauding—little four- and five-year-olds in the front row, youngsters in the second and third grades, older children, teen-agers, high school seniors, teachers, perhaps five hundred people in all—and all applauding vociferously. But it was the children who were applauding the loudest and longest! In my fifty years in the business, I have never heard anything like it. They applauded so long I began to feel embarrassed and tried to wave them to stop. When that didn't work, I began shouting over the tumult "Children, please ... please! Please stop! Don't you realize what you're *doing*? You're spoiling an old man!"

This brought a fresh burst of applause, but finally they quieted down long enough for me to say

"Boys and girls, I just celebrated my seventy-fifth birthday a couple of weeks ago, and I wonder if you beautiful children would mind singing the Happy Birthday song for me just one more time? Would you do that?"

Would they! Those fresh young voices nearly rocked the walls they sang with such fervor and enthusiasm, and when they finished, I said, "Children ... I've heard that song many, many times in my lifetime, but I've never heard it sung like that! That's the best birthday present I've ever received. Now let me see if I can't try to find a way to thank you a little bit."

Jon had gotten my accordion out of the car, so I pulled it on and, for the next half hour, put on a "one-man show." I played some of the waltzes and polkas I had learned while growing up on the farm near Strasburg, North Dakota, when I was just about the age of the smallest children present. I played requests. I answered questions about our Musical Family. At one point, I played a polka and dragged an unwilling Jon out on the floor to dance with some of the girls. That was a mistake, I want to tell you! Poor Jon tried hard, but it was pretty obvious he had never danced the polka before, as he bounced and hopped around the floor to screams of laughter from the audience. Watching him dance made me want to have a waltz myself, but there was no one to play the accordion. So I improvised— something I've become rather expert at over the years— and had the crowd start clapping in time to a waltz rhythm. "ONE, two, three; ONE, two, three," I sang, instructing them to accent the "ONE." When they had the beat down pat, I handed my baton over to a handsome little boy named Bruce Loy in the front row, and asked him to keep on "leading" while I danced with the girls. He was only about five years old, but he did such a good job that he got a big round of applause, too. Later I gave him the baton to keep as a souvenir. His eyes got enormous. He took the baton and held it to him very gently, and I heard later on that he took it to bed with him that night.

What a glorious morning that was! Just unbelievable. I don't know if rural youngsters are our strongest fans or not—chances are they watch the show with their parents—but I do know that they made it plain that they felt very, very close to us and wanted to let us know about it.

I felt so happy to be with them, so relaxed, so downright lucky to have them as our friends. They were so clean, so wholesome, so sweet—so young! It was hard to tear myself away, but I knew they had to get back to class, and Jon and I had to be on our way. So finally I bowed—hands clasped together in the gesture of respect and affection German people often use—and walked out the door, waving my thanks as I went. And those bright and shining faces, that overwhelming strong, steady undiminished applause followed me all the way out to the street—filling the air, filling my ears, filling my heart.

Back in the car, I sat silently for a moment while Jon busied himself maneuvering us back onto the highway. Then I said, almost in wonder, "Jon, do you realize that if we hadn't stopped here for breakfast, I would have missed one of the great experiences of my lifetime?"

Jon smiled. "It was pretty nice," he agreed. "Those kids sure loved you."

"And I loved them. I had no idea we had that many young fans. From now on, I'm going to make sure we have numbers on every show, just for them."

"Good idea." Jon nodded and began driving swiftly down the highway towards Wichita, through the lovely farmlands which stretched for miles and miles on either side of the road. Neither of us said anything for perhaps a half mile or so. Then I said softly, "Jon—I want to tell you something. Meeting those youngsters today was something I will never, ever forget. It was a high spot. In fact—it was the high spot of my life."

3.

Let Them Work!

———————————————————————ↄↄ

Of course as I realized later, one of the reasons I had been moved so deeply by my meeting with the children of Macksville, was because of my great love and concern for all children today. I've always felt very close to young folks. Even when I was pretty young myself, I made it a point to develop youthful talent whenever I could. One of my first finds was a talented little boy named Bobby Beers, who had a voice twice as big as he was. (Some of you folks who knew us in the Dakotas during my early years may remember him. He did a sensational impression of Ted Lewis.) Later, in television, I found and developed the Lennon Sisters, who eventually became America's Sweethearts of Song. Janet was only nine and a half when I began working with the girls, and I still look on the ensuing twelve years as one of the nicest times in my life. It was through the girls that I met their uncles, Ted and Jack Lennon, who have since become my indispensable right-hand men, so my meeting with the Lennons turned out to be a bonus all the way around.

In more recent years, you may recall the Semonski Sisters who were with us for three-and-a-half years, and the current crop of youngsters who decorate our show: lovely Mary Lou Metzger, who never never never lets me down—we all love her; multi-talented Gail Farrell, who has developed from a group chorus singer to a soloist, a pianist, and an arranger—I have such high regard for the way she has developed her potential; our beautiful Anacani, who's become one of the most loved and most popular stars we've ever had; handsome Tom Netherton, who was "given" to us by Sheila and Harold Schafer (Tom was singing in their Medora, North Dakota, resort—"but he's too good for us, he belongs on your show, he belongs to the nation!" Sheila and Harold told us.) Then there is Ava Barber, from Knoxville, Tennessee, fast becoming one of the most popular country singers in the nation, and rightfully so—no one has ever been more cooperative than Ava and her husband, Roger; Kathie Sullivan who, in my opinion, has one of the loveliest, purest voices I've ever heard— and also a tremendous sense of humor which we all enjoy; and of course our new quartet, the darling little sisters, Sheila and Sherry Aldridge, who are so dependable and talented; and two of the nicest young men I've ever met in my life, the Otwell twins, David and Roger. Everybody loves them. And so would you.

All these youngsters are as different as night and day, and all as close to me as if they were my own children. When I tell you folks that helping each of them overcome certain obstacles and achieve stardom on their own makes me just as happy as it makes them, I'm really understating the case. I am just filled with pride and pleasure, the kind a father feels when his son or daughter wins the gold medal at school, or places first in a talent contest. They are happy too, of course, but I honestly believe that the measure of happiness for me—the person who helps them succeed—is even greater. That's one of the messages I want to convey strongly in this book, to any businessman who might be considering adopting our success methods. So I'll say it again. If any of you business people are looking for a way to bring more joy and meaning into your life, you can do it best by helping a young person develop his potential!

But it's becoming more and more difficult to do this, and it's hurting our youngsters. I've often said that if we hope to make this country stronger and better—indeed if we hope to save it at all—then we must begin with our young people. It's to our own best interests to develop their potential in every possible way, but so far I'm afraid we're not doing a very good job of it.

They are probably the brightest, healthiest, strongest young Americans in history, and they should be so engrossed with all the good things of life that our crime and vandalism rates would be almost wiped out; our teen-age mental illness virtually nonexistent; and our youth unemployment rates at a minimal level. Unfortunately, as you and I know only too well, not one of those things is so.

Instead, hundreds of thousands of them are languishing on street corners, unable—and finally, unwilling—to get a job. Hundreds of thousands more are trapped in jobs they neither wanted nor are suited for—unhappy, discouraged, constantly frustrated in their attempts to fulfill their potential, forced to waste the precious, precious years of their youth. And that is just not right.

However, I'm basically an optimist, and I'm

convinced there *is* a way to solve every single one of those problems. In fact, I know there's a way—because we've been using it for years in our orchestra.

And the way? Well, knowing me, you may not be too surprised to learn that it begins with work! But I'm absolutely convinced, through a lifetime of experience and observation, that the best answer to every single problem that plagues our young people today is simply to let—them—work!

But that brings up the real problem, because in our society today, we don't allow our young folks to work. With the best intentions in the world, we've arranged things so millions of them can't work, even when they want to. By the time we finally say, "Okay, now you're old enough to go to work and start taking care of yourselves," they haven't the slightest notion how to go about it.

Now, I told you in the preface of this book that I was going to make some very specific recommendations as to how we could best help our young people improve the quality of their lives. I also told you that some of my suggestions might surprise you a little, maybe even shock you. Well, you better get ready, because here comes my first recommendation. And it's this:

> *I believe the best thing we can do to help our younger generation today is to get rid of the one law that has been holding them back the most—and that's the child labor law.*

> *I believe we should repeal it—abolish it— whatever you want to call it. Just get rid of it—and give our young people the right to work again.*

Does that shock you a little? I must admit that when I first began suggesting repeal of the child labor law, I got an almost unanimous reaction from my listeners—stark horror! "But how would you protect youngsters?" they wanted to know. "How would you keep employers from abusing them?" My friends, business acquaintances, neighbors, even the girls in the office began looking at me as if they'd never before realized what a monster I was. Here I was, someone they had always thought was fair-minded and reasonable, wanting to make young children work!

But after I explained I didn't want to *make* them work—only *allow* them to do so, if they wished; and after I explained my specific objections to the child labor law, I generally got another reaction. People would look surprised and say, "Well, I never thought of it that way. Maybe you're right."

I don't think this happened because I spoke with such persuasive skill, or even because I was the boss. I think it was simply because I pointed out some facts they had never considered before. Let me repeat them for you here: The child labor law was passed, if my mind serves me correctly, in 1935, because certain employers had been exploiting and even abusing young children, and something had to be done about it. We all agreed on that. But the child labor law was not the answer. Instead of punishing the employers who had caused the problem, it punished the innocent young-sters!—by taking away their inborn right to work. And instead of helping young people prepare for life by getting the training and jobs they needed, the child labor law made it just about impossible.

If the law had made life any better for our youngsters, I would never question it. Not at all. No one wants to help young people any more than I do—it's become the driving force of my life. But let me ask you something. Is life any better for our teen-agers since the law was passed? Are they any happier, more calm and stable, more confident about the future? Are the crime rates for young people down? The unemployment rates? Most of the time, I'm afraid the answer is no. In my opinion, the child labor law not only did not help them—it harmed them. It made it difficult for them to get jobs in the professions that interested them most, at just the time in their life when they could learn the quickest and best. And if that's not harming them, I don't know what is!

Now, I realize of course, that young people can get jobs under the age of eighteen with a work permit. But very few employers want to get involved in more paper work or more government controls—they probably have more than enough already! Also, very few employers are anxious to pay young people a minimum wage before they've even learned how to work. What that really means is that the overwhelming majority of our young people have trouble getting jobs or training until they're eighteen. Then they can't get jobs because they have no experience! It just doesn't make sense.

Our kids need to work. Work is the best tool they'll ever have to help them build strong, happy, productive lives. So let's stop punishing them. Let's allow them to work.

Maybe you think "letting them work" is too simple an answer, too pat. Well, let me just say that "work" is the reason I'm here today! Work is the reason our whole show is here. The people in our orchestra, almost without exception, are great believers in work. Moreover, almost every one of them, including me, has been working hard and constantly since early childhood, and for the life of me, I can't see that it's hurt any of us a bit!

Let me just give you a few examples: Joe Livoti, our superb first violinist, was taken by his father to hear the great Jascha Heifetz play. The auditorium was so jammed that Joe, who was still very small, and his father had to sit up on stage, close to where the great master performed. Young Joe was so enthralled listening to the glorious tones, that he was inspired to learn to play the violin himself. He worked so hard that by the age of twelve he had won a scholarship to the Boston Conservatory of Music (and another when he was fourteen). His early years were filled with hard constant daily practice and work—but does he regret it? "Regret it?" asks Joe in astonishment. "No! It gave me a goal in life and prepared me for the job I love more than anything else. I'm grateful for it!"

Russ Klein, our fine saxophone man, has a similar story. By the time he was fourteen years old, he had become good enough to form his own little band, and he and his schoolmates played for dances after school and on weekends. I guess maybe the child labor law wasn't around in those days, because Russ carried a full load of schoolwork, too, It certainly wasn't easy— but did it hurt him? I don't think so. On the contrary, that concentrated early hard work made him into one of the best professionals in the country—and also into one of the happiest men I know.

There are many, many other examples in the band—over fifty if you count me, and you'd better! But

just take a look. Myron Floren worked, and worked
hard, on the family farm back in Webster, South
Dakota. He tells me he practiced two hours on the
accordion every day before he went to school, came
home and helped with the farm chores, and then
practiced hours after dinner every night. I guess no one
in that little town had heard about the child labor law
either, because Myron was safe. And did all that hard
work hurt him? Well, today Myron is the best all-
around accordionist in the world, as well as being a
respected, successful, happy man. So I guess it didn't
hurt him too much.

Bob Havens, our superb slide-trombone man,
acknowledged to be one of the finest Dixieland jazz
artists in the nation, was only six years old when he
began studying violin. Later he switched to trombone,
and by the age of ten was playing in the "family band"
at lawn socials and ball games, and at twelve, in another
small band which played for local dances. He also
performed with the local Quincy, Illinois, symphony,
while carrying a full load of schoolwork. Did all that
work hurt him? I once asked Bob that very question.
"No!" he said instantly. "No way! I enjoyed it, and it all
came so easily to me then. When you're young, you
grasp things quickly and they stick with you." (I agree
completely.)

And then there's Henry Cuesta, the man with
the golden clarinet. He's another who started studying
violin at age six, switching to the clarinet at nine. He,
too, played in small bands and performed with the local
symphony in Corpus Christi, Texas, before he was out
of high school. Did that hurt him? I doubt it. He was
recently awarded a gold clarinet by the Selmer Corporation in recognition of his great artistry—I would say

Henry is one of the finest clarinet men in the nation, if not the world. He's also one of the happiest of men, with a family life most people only dream about— warm, close, loving, the old-fashioned kind of family which works and plays together. (Except when he's practicing! "Then," says his wife, Janette, "Henry disappears into the little studio he's built at home. We hear him, but we don't see him for hours at a time.")

All these men practice at least an hour a day, or two or three. All of them are preeminent in their field. And all are unanimous in their belief that unless they'd been given the privilege of hard, sustained work in their early years, they might never have made it to the top. Their days were long and full of hard work, that's true. But it gave them something to work *for*—and they discovered, early in life, the tremendous exhilaration, the great satisfaction, that comes from stretching your- self and discovering your potential—and then working to develop it!

WORK

WORK can help young people find out what they want to do in life. If we don't let them try various jobs, how are they going to find out?

WORK can help them develop the skills and traits necessary for success in life.

WORK can help them develop stamina and patience, make realistic judgments, learn how to get along with people, put a little cash in their pockets, and teach them the value of money.

WORK can keep them out of trouble!

But there are intangible benefits that come from work which are even more important. There's something inspiring, satisfying, almost ennobling about doing a job thoroughly and well. You feel good about the job, good about yourself. Our teen-agers desperately need to experience that feeling, need to develop the confidence that is so important in life.

Work can also help you physically. Just look at me! Here I am, an old man of seventy-six—at least the calendar tells me so—but I still play eighteen holes of golf at a time, occasionally walking much of the way. And never in the world could I do so if I hadn't developed strong leg muscles in my youth. I pushed a plow for miles and miles behind our team of horses, breaking up the North Dakota earth. I wasn't too thrilled about it at the time. But oh, what benefits I was storing up for myself! I was laying the groundwork for the good health I enjoy today.

I've always felt that denying a young person a chance to work is really denying him a chance at life; and if you think I'm being too dramatic when I say that, then just consider this: Most of us have to work for a living—that's just a plain hard fact of life. If our young people are going to have to work eventually, then why not help them find work they will enjoy—even love? In my opinion that's the secret of happiness, and I don't have to look any farther than myself to find an example. I *love* my work, thank God every day I have it, and thank my parents for giving me the privilege of finding it when I was still young enough to do something about it. My parents gave me love, religious faith, music—and work. Love gave me the security I needed. Religion gave me rules to live by. Music gave me my goal in life. But *work* helped me realize it! Work is the answer to so many of the problems facing our young people today that I think we owe it to them—to ourselves—and to our nation, to make it available to them. We can do it best by removing the legal restrictions that are holding them back.

Work is not a curse! It's a blessing—and a blessing we have kept from our young folks for much too long.

Part Two

Our Musical Family

4.

The Need for Discipline

Well as you may have gathered by now—I love work! In fact I'm sometimes teased about my devotion to it. "You ought to spell your name "Work" instead of Welk!" my writer, Bernice, said to me one day. (This was in the final stages of meeting the deadline on our book, I must admit.) But I didn't mind. If there were nothing else I could do for our young people except make it possible for them to understand and enjoy the benefits of work, I'd feel I had left them a priceless legacy.

But of course there are many other attributes that help in building a truly fulfilled life, and one of the most important of these is discipline, or, to be more specific, self-discipline. And that seems to be so very, very hard for us human beings to achieve! Ask any smoker who's trying to kick the habit. Or any drinker, or someone who's chronically late, or eats too much, or lies or cheats, or does something else deeply ingrained into him. It's ofttimes nearly impossible to correct such habits once they become embedded in you, and that's

just another reason I'm such a believer in early training
and discipline.

I really feel so very fortunate that my brothers
and sisters and I were all taught, early in life, to
discipline ourselves. We did our assigned chores on the
farm when the chores were scheduled—and not when
we felt like doing them. We got up every morning at
daybreak, too, not because we wanted to, but because
that was the only way we could get our day's work done.
I still recall very vividly the time I got the whole family
up by myself. I was pretty young at the time, but I
evidently wanted to be "leader of the group" even in
those years. So when the light streamed into the
sleeping loft I shared with my brothers and awakened
me, I decided to take over the responsibility of getting
everyone up for the day. I went around from bed to bed,
shaking my sleeping brothers. "Time to get up!" I
caroled. "It's morning, c'mon everybody. Up, up, up!"
Groans of disbelief greeted this announcement. "Go
'way," muttered my brother Louis, "it can't be time
yet!" "Oh, yes it is," I said virtuously. "C'mon now, get
up!" Then I went downstairs and repeated the whole
performance for my sisters. "Time to get up, girls," I
sang cheerfully. "It's morning, better start breakfast!"
More groans and sighs came from the girls, but they
dutifully got up. I went out to the barn with my
brothers and got the horses fed and watered and hitched
up for the day, and then we went back to the kitchen
where the girls had cooked the usual big farm breakfast—bacon, eggs, sausage, German-fried potatoes,
homemade bread, jams, jellies, milk, coffee, cinnamon-
and-sugar coffee cake. We all sat eating silently for a few
minutes, concentrating on our food, when suddenly the
clock in the living room began to strike. "Boing!" We

looked up and waited. And waited. But no more "boings." To my intense embarrassment, it was only one o'clock in the morning! The bright moonlight had fooled me completely.

Well I want to tell you things came flying at me from all around the table for the next few seconds, and the family never did let me live that down. But after the first few howls of outrage and threats of bodily harm, everyone burst into laughter. The girls cleared the table, and the boys and I went back to the barn and took the harness off the surprised horses, who surely must have been thinking what a short day *that* was; and then we all went back to bed for a few more hours' sleep. Everybody but me. I went back to bed, but not to sleep. Once again I'd demonstrated beyond all doubt that I was the undisputed dummer-esel of the family.

But to get back to discipline. I'm of the opinion that self-discipline gives you a handle to keep your life under control and achieve far more joy and happiness than you could otherwise. Our television show is a wonderful example of what I mean. There is just no way in the world that we could get our show on the air without discipline. When you have an orchestra of more than fifty people, many of whom perform in solo spots; and when you have an hour long television show which is performed straight through, with no stops whatever; and when your shows include eighteen to twenty different numbers each week, then you need an incredible amount of self-discipline and cooperation. We tape our show in one day, which is just about unheard of in TV. I'm proud of that record and I thought you might like to know how we do it, so I'm going to tell you from beginning to end. If you're a good student, you may pick up so many pointers about how to produce a TV show, you may want to start your own band! At any rate, this is the way we put our show together, from the moment we first think about it, till the time you see it on the air.

———————————————————————————————————— ♫

I might tell you that each show begins as an idea at a production meeting in the conference room of our office in Santa Monica. There are nine of us involved in these meetings: Jim Hobson, producer-director; George Cates, musical director; Jack Imel, assistant director; Bob Ballard, chief arranger and choral director; Joe Rizzo, Curt Ramsey, and Jack Pleis, arranging staff; George Thow, writer and production assistant; and me.

We sit around our small conference room, with plenty of coffee to keep us going (tea, for me), and talk over possible themes and songs for the show. I have to laugh. For years I tried to teach the fellows what was best for the show. I guess I taught them too well. Now, they're telling me! All nine of us have strong opinions, and we've had our differences over the years as we've tried to cope with the different types of music that came our way. But in the main, we've managed to stick close to our original goal—playing beautiful melodies, with a good dance beat, in the style the composer had in mind when he originally wrote the piece.

Once we've settled on the theme and music for the show, the arrangers get to work arranging it; the singers begin learning their songs at home; Rose Weiss, our wonderful costume designer, starts preparing appropriate costumes; and our scenic designer, Charles Koon, begins constructing sets. And on the Thursday preceding the actual taping, the whole cast gets together for the first rehearsal. This is standard procedure for each show, and we generally adhere to the following rehearsal schedule:

First Rehearsal: Thursday

ANNEX STUDIO: 1032 N. Sycamore Street, Hollywood, California
Rehearsal Call: 10:00 A.M.

The Annex Studio is a landmark in Hollywood, and we've recorded there for so long it's become a second home for us. On Thursdays it really looks that way, with "Welk-people" arriving every few minutes from nine o'clock on. You might see Tom Netherton drive up and unwind his six-foot-five inches of talent from his little Datsun 280, or Bobby Burgess zooming up in his bright red Corvette or even me, in my sporty new Dodge. I don't go to many of these sessions, just enough to keep my fingers on the pulse!

Long before ten o'clock our engineer, Thorne (Thorney) Nogar, is ready in the sound booth, the fellows have all their music stacked in order on their music racks, and George Cates is standing at the podium, raring to go. There are twenty-five men in our orchestra, and when George raises his baton at precisely 10:00 A.M., there are fifty eyes glued on him in total concentration.

I just wish you folks could see George in action. It's really something to see! He paces up and down the studio floor like a caged tiger, cueing first one section and then another, beaming with delight if the

music sounds good, scowling fiercely if it doesn't.
George can hear a sour note through twenty-four other
instruments and shout immediately "Trombones!
Change your E flat to an E natural, B flat to a B
natural!" faster than you can say yes or no. I marvel at
his musical ear and technical knowledge.

He's made a tremendous improvement in my
band. I don't want to sound as if I'm bragging, but I
honestly believe that George and his staff have created
for me the best all-around band the world has ever seen,
from the standpoint of being able to play any type or
style of music—sweet, swing, country, Dixieland, jazz,
disco, or concert. I'm deeply grateful to him. When I
first found him, he was musical director for Coral and
Decca records, after having worked with Ben Bernie,
Dick Stabile, Henry Busse, and Russ Morgan. I found
out only recently, by the way, that George and my
manager, Sam Lutz, were once roommates, back in the
days when they both worked with Henry Busse. What
a small world. George was a musical prodigy who
played violin at the age of six, and later studied to
become a lawyer at New York University. But the lure
of music was too strong, and he decided to devote his
life to it. And am I glad!

While George is busy rehearsing the band in
the main studio, Bob Ballard is coaching the singers in
another, and the arrangers are working in their small,
cozy office, situated next to the music library. I might
tell you that we worked so many years at the Annex—
not only rehearsing the show, but also recording all our
albums—that the Annex management built us a music
library at the studio so we could keep all our arrangements right where we need them. It makes for a highly
efficient arrangement.

The Thursday rehearsal ends anywhere from six to seven or more hours after it begins—however long it takes to get each number thoroughly rehearsed. It's a long day but an exciting one, the first time we hear the arrangements and songs come to life so we can judge the sound or the "feel" and make any necessary changes. It's hard on George. He is frequently on his feet for ten hours on Thursday, and "Thursdays," he sighs, "are the days I go home and collapse!" But he loves it.

Second Rehearsal: Monday

CBS STUDIO: Rehearsal Hall "E" and Studio 31
Fairfax and Beverly, Hollywood,
California

Rehearsal Call: 11:00 A.M.

Monday we take one more step in our countdown to show time. The performers check in first for fittings on their costumes with Rose Weiss, in her big and airy workroom on the second floor. If you ever get a chance to visit Rose's warehouse of costumes, you really should take advantage of it. She's been collecting gowns and theatrical costumes for years, and has rows and rows and rows of them hanging from triple racks from the floor to the ceiling of her oversized wardrobe room. I would say the room is at least twenty feet high and is equipped with rolling ladders to reach the clothes on the highest racks. Each performer's clothes hang in separate, labeled sections; shoes and slippers are all neatly boxed and tagged; and every tie or hankie or feather boa is color-coded and cross-referenced to its matching suit or gown. It's kind of a dazzling sight when you first walk in—you see racks of beautiful full-skirted waltz gowns in one section, country square-dance in another; colorful jeweled dance costumes, Hawaiian outfits, Easter bunny suits—I think Rose has an outfit for every day in the year! And the amazing thing (to me, anyway) is that she and her devoted staff know exactly where everything is, and when you're dealing with literally thousands of costumes for over fifty people, that's pretty wonderful. But so is Rose Weiss.

Monday is also the day Bob Ballard works with the choral groups and any individual soloist who needs or requests help. Jack Pleis plays the piano for these sessions—the band is excused for the day.

Then on Monday afternoon there's a "walk-through" rehearsal of the entire show in Studio 31—and this is Jim Hobson's territory. I'm really at a loss when I try to describe what he does. All I can tell you is that Jim works on the show constantly in his head, and when he directs a rehearsal or taping, it's just one more step in the continuing creative process he goes through twenty-four hours a day, seven days a week. Where he gets his unending stream of ideas, I can't imagine. During the course of twenty-four years on nationwide TV, we've had to repeat certain popular songs from time to time, but always Jim comes through with a new way to present them.

He once took me downstairs in CBS to the video department to show me how he edits our show after we tape it. I took one look at that maze of wall-to-wall lights and buttons and flashing dials and little red beepers and said, "Jim, I'll let you take total responsibility for this, it's way over my head! I'll stay in the music department." He's superb at handling the myriad of camera angles and cues called for in each show—he may throw as many as four hundred different cues in each show, but it's his creative genius and sensitivity in working with people, plus his genuine musical "feel" that are so valuable to me. And I'm going to put in another plug for early training right here! Like George, Jim knew from his earliest years what he wanted to be. He was so eager to get a job in TV that he hung around constantly, taking any job he could get—sweeping floors, whatever. If he couldn't get a job, then he hid behind scenery flats to watch the action, just soaking up knowledge. He was still a very young man when we hired him as assistant to our producer, Ed Sobol, but he was so good that when Mr. Sobol passed on in 1962, we made Jim our full producer-director. He has more than justified every hope I ever had for him.

Well, that may give you some idea of how I feel about my right-hand people! But to continue, on Monday afternoon Jack Imel helps Jim direct a walk-through of the show, and if there are scenes involving lots of people and action—maybe a group dance number or county fair or some such thing—then the rehearsal can get quite complicated.

But by late afternoon on Monday, every song has been rehearsed, all the action has been blocked-out, every costume is ready (or in the process of being completed) and all is in readiness for "T" day, Tape Day—Tuesday—my day! That's the high spot of my week, the day everything comes together. And it starts bright and early. For me, it starts around 5:00 A.M.

TAPE DAY!

"T" DAY: Tuesday

CBS STUDIO: Studio 31
                    Fairfax and Beverly, Hollywood,
                    California

Rehearsal Call: 10:00 A.M.

Rehearsal may be set for 10:00 A.M., but I've been up
since five or earlier, had my swim, hit a bucket of golf
balls in my back yard, eaten a good breakfast prepared
by my wife, Fern, in anticipation of a long day, gone to
the office, done a little work, and then picked up Laurie
Rector and Henry Cuesta at 8:15 for our trip cross-town
to CBS. Laurie is my new secretary (she's Lois' sister—
Lois is now our executive secretary, heading my staff of
four very efficient and lovely young ladies), and Henry
Cuesta lives so close to our office that I generally pick
him up on the way into town too. The three of us arrive
about 9:00 A.M., park in the artists' parking lot at CBS,
and head immediately for Studio 31 on the second floor.
          It's usually quiet when we push open the door
of the huge studio. The only sound to be heard is the
plink-plink of a piano tuner hard at work out on the
sound stage. That always brings back memories of the
days when my little band and I used to play in small-
town ballrooms in the Midwest. Nearly always the
piano was out of tune, and there was seldom a piano
tuner around, so I finally took a piano tuning course at
the McPhail School of Music in Minneapolis and
learned how to do the job myself.
          Laurie unpacks her typewriter and settles
down at a big desk in my dressing room, a pleasant and

efficient three-room suite consisting of a sitting room, makeup room, and small bath and clothes closet. George Thow arrives with his cue cards to set up shop in the makeup room. I walk around greeting early arrivals—Kenny Trimble and Barney Liddell, who are always there early, and Myron Floren, of course. If you don't see him, you can certainly hear him noodling away on his accordion. One by one the kids begin to arrive, with the fellows going immediately to their places on the bandstand to tune up their instruments. Now the "plink-plink" of the piano is joined by the "thunk-thunk" of the bass fiddle, a few sweet runs from the saxophones, and maybe a violin cadenza or two. When I hear the familiar mixture of sounds, my heart starts to quicken, and I can scarcely wait for the rehearsal to begin.

By the time Jim Rice, the floor director, takes over the intercom to announce "FIFTEEN MIN-UTES!" almost everyone has arrived. At "FIVE MIN-UTES" everybody's there (or they better be!). And just before ten, Jim Hobson's voice comes over the loud-speaker from the control room "Okay, kids, we're ready. Five, four, three, two, one—GO!" George gives the band the downbeat—and the rehearsal begins.

That's when I go to work! Bernice spent a full day with us getting notes for this book, and I thought her observations of what went on during our day-long taping might be of interest to you. So here is what she had to say about us. Okay, Bernice—it's all yours!

"Lawrence" (wrote Bernice) "sits in a big white plush armchair in his dressing room, and never takes his eyes off the large closed-circuit color TV built into the paneled wall opposite him, perhaps fifteen feet away. The phone rings constantly and people drop into the office all day long, and Lawrence always manages to be friendly and cordial. But his full attention is really riveted on that screen, monitoring the rehearsal out on the stage, and he knows exactly what's going on every second.

"There's a special telephone on a table to his left, with a row of colored lights in its base—green for Jim Hobson in the control room; yellow for Bob Ballard in the sound booth; blue for George Cates on stage. Lawrence is on the phone often, calling one or another of them to change tempo, or simplify the orchestration, or just tell them everything sounds fine and needs no change.

"On this particular morning (January 3, 1979, the first show after a two-week Christmas vacation), everybody in the band found occasion to come by at least once and wish Lawrence a Happy New Year. Ed Kletter, head of the J. B. Williams Advertising Agency which has sponsored the show for nineteen years, had shipped a huge box filled with their products—Aqua Velva, Rose Milk, Lectric Shave, Geritol, etc., and Lawrence had set them all out on a table. Whenever anyone came in, Lawrence talked with them warmly and urged them to take their pick of the gifts. It was nice. There is obviously friendship between him and the members of the band, real and warm—honest affection that shows up very clearly.

"Precisely at 10:00 A.M. the band and singers and dancers start rehearsing the opening number, 'Love Is Sweeping the Country,' and Lawrence watches the action intently on the monitoring screen. It looks and sounds fine to me, but after about eight bars, Lawrence is on his feet, out the door, and on stage in conference with George. 'It's too slow, George,' he says, 'too draggy. Let's lift the tempo a little,' and he snaps his fingers to indicate the tempo he wants.

"George nods, but the three dancers—Bobby Burgess, Arthur Duncan, and Jack Imel—protest that they need the slow tempo for the type of steps they do in the number.

" 'But fellows,' expostulates Lawrence, 'the number's dying this way! C'mon, let's instill a little pep! Could you do it double-time?'

"The boys confer, try the routine in double-time, and start smiling, because the results are fantastic! The improvement in the whole number was really spectacular and seemed even more so to me, because it seemed good to start with.

"Mary Lou dashes into the dressing room next for a quick rehearsal of her number for the following week, a takeoff of 'Oh, Johnny!' She went right down on her haunches, like a little puppy in the crowded dressing room, and sang it with big eyes and much expression. Lawrence listened, eyes bright, following every nuance, and when she finished he said, 'That's wonderful! ... but listen, Mary Lou—Wee Bonnie did more like this!' And *he* proceeded to sing it with big eyes and much expression! Mary Lou collapsed in laughter. 'Listen,' she said finally, 'I wasn't even alive when Wee Bonnie Baker sang it!' Nevertheless, she caught what he wanted and went out the door singing 'Ooooh, Johnny' in a wee little voice.

"Up on the TV screen Anacani is singing, 'Love Me with All Your Heart.' Afterward she sticks her head in the dressing room door and Lawrence compliments her, first on her performance, and then on her choice of husband. Anacani glows.

"Next up is Ralna, and Lawrence works with her on her interpretation of 'It Had to Be You.' She comes through with a gorgeous rendition. What a talent she is. Lawrence says she sounds very much like the best of the girl band-singers in the Big Band days. Whenever he talks with her or anyone else on the show, he's quick to interject a suggestion about some future goal—a record album, a personal appearance, a new number. He never fails to compliment or thank someone for a good job, and also set up a future exciting project. As a motivator he's a past master!

"Bobby Burgess brings in his dancing-partner-of-the-day, Elaine Niverson of Houston, Texas, a very pretty girl, and Lawrence makes her feel right at home. 'Let's see if she's as good as you say, Bobby,' he says, and begins waltzing around the dressing room with her. They sail around the coffee table and back again to Bobby who watches, grinning. 'She'll do,' says Lawrence, handing her back to Bob. 'In fact, she's better than you said!' Elaine flushes with pleasure, and then she and Bobby go out on stage and do a spectacular tango number.

"Then the quartet (the Otwells and the Aldridges) run into trouble. The song they had originally scheduled wasn't cleared in time for the taping, so they are singing a number they had learned earlier, 'Shenandoah.' Again, it sounded okay to me—but not to Lawrence! He was on the phone immediately to Jim, 'Ask the kids to come and see me, will you, please?' In a few minutes all four youngsters, looking a little worried, come in; and Lawrence goes to work with them, explaining exactly how their phrasing and intonation could be improved. He's very gentle with them, but very specific as to what he wants. It's almost eerie to watch the changes coming into the number as they work. At the end of twenty minutes, they had gotten the feel of the song exactly. Again, the improvement was remarkable.

"Up on the TV monitor Arthur Duncan is dancing to 'Now's the Time to Fall in Love.' No changes necessary. Ken Delo does 'What Are You Doing for the Rest of Your Life.' Again, no change. Ava comes on looking like a glamorous singing star from the neck down in a hot pink beaded floor-length gown—and looking not-so-glamorous from the neck up, with her hair in curlers. Rose Weiss stands on stage watching like a hawk for hems that need shortening or buttons that need tightening. She doesn't miss a thing!

"Suddenly, we have a little drama on stage. Barney Liddell, who has been with the band for thirty-one years, is playing a trombone solo, a number entitled, 'I Don't Know Why.' He looks rather strange as he does so, because he keeps peering over his right shoulder and looking down at the floor as he plays. When the camera pulls back, we can see why. Barney has spread his sheet music on the floor and keeps sneaking little peeks at it. Lawrence takes one look at this sight and is out the door like a shot. (He rarely walks, nearly always moves at a half-jog.) He advances resolutely on Barney, who stands there looking as guilty as a small boy caught with his hand in the cookie jar. 'Boss,' says Barney immediately, 'I don't know why I did that ... uh ... ' He voice trails off as Lawrence just stands there, regarding him. Barney tries again. 'Listen, Boss,' he flounders ... 'listen, I *do* know the song ... I just put the music on the floor for assurance ... I—I don't know why ... ' Lawrence shakes his head.

'Barney,' he says finally, 'I DON'T KNOW WHY you put it there either. In fact, I DON'T KNOW WHY I hired you in the first place!' At this the whole band breaks up, while Barney assures Lawrence he will have the number down letter-perfect by show time. Looking very solemn and contrite, he picks the music up off the floor, puts it away, and then plays the solo again—perfectly.

"At one o'clock everybody breaks for lunch—everyone except Lawrence, who beds down on the sofa in his dressing room with two pillows and a light blanket. When we come back an hour later, he sits up, yawns, blinks his eyes, and says, 'Oh, I had such a good nap! I fell asleep about ten seconds after you left.' What a blessing to be able to do that.

"Rehearsal proceeds swiftly, with Lawrence working intently on each number and at 4:45, it comes to an end. With ten minutes out of each hour as a rest period for the musicians, plus an hour and ten minutes at lunch, this means the entire show has been rehearsed in about five hours. There were no great changes in any of the numbers—it was more a matter of heightening, intensifying, shading, getting the tempo exactly right to bring out the best in each number. To me it was an exhibition of what can happen when a master is in charge. In each case Lawrence seemed to know exactly where the trouble spot was, and how to fix it. All those years of paying his dues pay off on this one day when he can go right through twenty numbers, one after another, and know instantly whether they're right or not.

"His taste and judgment seem infallible. People come to him all day long for advice and direction, the entire show revolves around him, and all the final decisions are his.

"At five o'clock, Lawrence walks out on stage to chat with the dress rehearsal audience which has gathered to watch the dress rehearsal, and I go up into the control room where Jim is king, to watch the action. It reminds me of the engine room in a vast ship. There is tension here, tremendous tension! Jim sits in a swivel chair at a long desk with his assistants on either side, and every few seconds all through the show he calls out the number of the next camera angle he wants. The lighting in the control booth is soft, almost like glamorous stage lighting. But the atmosphere is super-tense! When you're dealing with split-second timing and decisions that can't be revoked without a great deal of trouble, the pressures are enormous. But Jim stays cool.

"The dress rehearsal reveals that the show is two minutes and twenty seconds too long, which means a conference on how to cut it. Jim and his assistants, Don Buccola and Lynne Warfel, head for Lawrence's dressing room, where Jim and Lawrence begin going right through the show, discussing where to cut a few seconds here, a few more there. Someone suggests cutting the first eight bars of Henry Cuesta's brilliant solo. 'How much will that cut?' Lawrence wants to know. 'Wait a minute!' George Cates begins singing the eight bars in a large loud baritone (which will never get him on the Welk show), while George Thow times him. 'Twelve seconds,' announces George Thow after Cates finishes his 'solo.'

"Silence reigns for a moment. Then almost simultaneously everyone agrees it would be better to cut one number which runs exactly two minutes and twenty seconds, than to cut bits and pieces of others.

"That much settled, Jim and the others dash out for dinner. Lawrence nibbles on a banana, a little yogurt, and drinks a carton of milk. His makeup man, Nick Schillace, turns up right on the dot of seven, and Lawrence climbs into his barber chair to get made up. Then he starts to get dressed in his stage clothes, which Rose has hanging in his closet—rose-beige vested suit with pale green hankie tucked in the pocket, dark maroon suede and patent leather shoes with socks tucked inside, a green tie hanging around the collar of a pale, pale green striped shirt. Lawrence first sits down to change his socks, but midway through peeling off his own black-ribbed stockings, he says appealingly, 'Rosie, do I have to change my socks? Nobody can see them, why can't I just leave them on?' He sticks out one black-clad foot. Rose gives him a look. 'Change them,' she orders, sounding just like a mother. 'Okay,' says Lawrence meekly, putting on the beige socks, 'you're the boss!'

"Dressed and looking very natty indeed, Lawrence emerges from his inner dressing room and Rose inspects him, stepping back to look him over from head to toe. 'Okay,' she says finally, 'you'll do.' Lawrence grins. 'Rose,' he says, picking up his baton and gazing at his pink and green reflection in the mirror, 'you've changed my whole image. The folks at home would never know me now!'"

"A brand new audience has assembled for the taping of the show itself, and Lawrence walks out onto the wide studio floor with the tiers of audience seats rising before him like bleachers. There is a sudden hum of recognition, and then a full-blown roar of approval and applause. Every seat is filled. There is a twelve-to-eighteen month wait for tickets to see this show, and the excitement level of the audience indicates how pleased they are to be at the taping.

"Lawrence chats with them like old friends, calls on Myron to play a waltz while he dances with some of the ladies from the audience, plays the accordion himself. He and Bob Warren, the show's announcer, do a little casual ad-libbing. Bob always regales the audience with a host of funny stories. He often introduces Lawrence by telling the audience that according to the Chamber of Commerce, there are three outstanding tourist attractions in Los Angeles. One of them is Disneyland. The other two are Forest Lawn— and Lawrence Welk. It always gets a big laugh.

"By five minutes to eight, everyone is waiting in the wings for the opening number, Jim is issuing last-minute orders from the control booth, and even the audience is caught up in the excitement. At five seconds to air time, Jim begins the countdown, 'FIVE, FOUR, THREE, TWO, ONE' and the show is on!

"And it's flawless. Not a mistake, Everything moves like a greased wheel, one performer doing a number on the right side of the stage, while the prop men quietly set up scenery on the left side. When the first singer finishes, the lights come up on the other side of the stage and the next performer begins. Everything moves like clockwork. One of the girls finishes a solo, and the moment she's off-camera, runs like a deer, off the stage and down the long hall to the girls' dressing room, where she jumps into a new costume and races back in time to join a group-singing number. This goes on all through the show.

"Lawrence leads the last number, 'Sweethearts on Parade,' an old Guy Lombardo favorite, a really rousing arrangement. The beat gets to him, and he begins dancing as he leads the band, beaming and smiling, completely taken over by the music! The audience loves it. They beam and smile too and burst into spontaneous applause.

"Then, it's 'Adios'—and the show is over.

"Lawrence thanks the audience, plods back to his dressing room, changes from his stage clothes into slacks and a shirt (only now does he begin to look tired), eats a carton of raspberry yogurt from the small dressing-room refrigerator, picks up his satchel, and at nine thirty heads out the door toward the parking lot and his car. It's been a long, long, long, long day."

When I finished reading Bernice's notes, I thought of a good many other details I could add, but I would say the essentials are all here. And when she compliments me so lavishly on my "taste" and "judgment," I can only say I've had the best teacher in the world—the audience. They've taught me so much, and any taste I've acquired over the years has come directly from them. Some of the lessons have been a little painful, but I'm grateful that they've told me very directly what they want, and how they want it, and what they don't want.

When we tape our show on Tuesday nights we start precisely at eight o'clock, and—barring accidents or breakdowns of some sort—keep going right through the whole show, exactly the way you see it on your television set, finishing up at nine o'clock. In that sense it's a live show—no retakes, no pauses in between numbers. With over fifty people in our cast, plus another couple of dozen in the background, we'd never be able to do that without total cooperation and—

discipline. Every person in the show has to discipline himself to learn songs thoroughly, to attend every rehearsal, to be on time for those rehearsals, to be ready and waiting and thoroughly prepared for each song cue, and give that little bit extra to insure the best possible show. I even have to discipline myself to keep the Dixieland jazz numbers to a minimum. If I had my way, we'd be playing them every week!

But our goal is to conceive and produce the most entertaining show we can; to please the audience, that is the paramount force in our lives. We want to do it. We love to do it. But we couldn't do it at all, except for one thing:

Discipline!

I thought perhaps you might be interested in what we call the "rundown" of our show, an outline of the numbers we play on a particular program. In this case, it's the Valentine show.

You'll notice a few penciled-in notations. In the first number "Hoopie" stands for Larry Hooper, who sang with the choral group. The notation "pic. of baby" after Sandi, Gail, and Mary Lou's number (9) indicates that we showed a photograph of Sandi's brand new baby, Emili, at that point. Numbers 9 and 14 were also switched, as you can see by the arrow—I just felt the show played better that way.

The Aldridges and Otwells' number was changed, as we mentioned, with the new number penciled in. (Yes, I know "Shenandoah" is spelled wrong. But I wanted you to see exactly how we operate, so here it is, misspellings and all.)

At the bottom of the page is the notation

```
PRE-REC: THURS, DEC. 21        8-S-22 (#388)      UNIF:  NEW BLUE

TAPE: WED, JAN. 3, '79                        "VALENTINE SHOW"
(STUDIO 43)
            LAWRENCE WELK SHOW 8-S-22 - AIR:  WEEK OF FEB. 8-14, 1979

BP 1.    LOVE IS SWEEPING THE COUNTRY       BAND & GROUP (Hoofie)
                                                         GRP.
   2.    OUR LOVE IS HERE TO STAY           BOB R & BAND

   3.    IT HAD TO BE YOU                   RALNA

         1ST COMM'L - A) J.B. WMS. - L.O. - B) J.B. WMS. - L.O.

   4.    LOVE ME WITH ALL YOUR HEART        ANACANI

   5.    NOW'S THE TIME TO FALL IN LOVE     ART

   6.    WHAT-DOING-REST OF LIFE            KEN

         2ND COMM'L - LOCAL (2 MINS.)

P  7.    BEAUTIFUL LOVE                     KATHIE

   8.    AMOR                               BOBBY & ELAINE NIVERSON

P 9A     WHAT THE WORLD NEEDS NOW           SANDI, GAIL, MARY L.

         3RD COMM'L - A) L.I. - BLOCK - B) L.I. - KELLOGG   (pic of
                                                             baby)
         --------------------STATION BREAK------------------------

   10.   A TIME FOR US                      BAND & GRP (G.C. COND)

   11.   I DON"T KNOW WHY                   JIM, BARNEY

   12.   JUST A LITTLE LOVIN'               AVA

         4TH COMM'L - A) L.I. - BLOCK - B) J.B. WMS. - L.O.

P 13.    SWEET DESIRE  SHENENDOAH           A'S & O'S

   14.   THIS IS MY SONG                    JOE F.

   15.   LOVER                              MYRON, BAND

P 16.    SPEAK TO ME OF LOVE (TCR)          NORMA

         5TH COMM'L - LOCAL (2 MINS.)

   17.   AND I LOVE YOU SO                  TOM

   18.   SWEETHEARTS ON PARADE              BAND

         6TH COMM'L - A) J.B. WMS. - L.O. - B) L.I. - HEET

         ADIOS & CLOSING
```

Guy - out
(Father ill)

"Guy—out (Father ill)." Guy had flown home to Tupelo, Mississippi, when his father became suddenly ill, and that's why Ralna was singing alone on that particular show.

Each of the key people in the show has a copy of this rundown—Jim, George Cates, Jack Imel, Rose Weiss, our art director Chuck Koon, George Thow, my secretary Laurie and me. There is also a rundown taped on the wall of every dressing room and in the makeup rooms, so that all of us know at all times just what our schedule is.

5.

Champagne and Geritol

If I seem dedicated to the idea of discipline, it's because I found out firsthand what can happen without it. After all these years I must now confess that there was one time when I lost control of the band completely. Not only that, I lost control of the audience, too.

It happened during the forties when the Miller High Life people were sponsoring us on their weekly nationwide radio show over the ABC network. The tie-up seemed like a natural—"The Champagne of Bottled Beer" sponsoring the "Champagne Music of Lawrence Welk." And it was wonderful, a tremendous boost for us. I've often felt that the Miller High Life people, and Fred Miller, opened the door for our future success, and I will always be deeply grateful to them.

In fact, I was so grateful at the time that I kept trying to find some way to express my thanks, and I finally decided to give them the band for one of their company parties. Everybody was very happy about this, including me. But I had forgotten one little detail. I had forgotten what the Miller High Life product was!

The evening started out well enough. We played champagne music for all we were worth, and the crowd danced with great enthusiasm. But as the evening wore on, they began checking on the quality of their product—just to make sure it was up to standard, I suppose—and before long, that crowd became the happiest I've ever seen, in a lifetime of happy crowds. The Miller High Life party just got higher and higher.

Then, at the first intermission, my boys got into the act too, returning to the bandstand flushed and very happy. A couple of them didn't return at all, and while I was still pondering what to do over this unexpected event, two of the guests solved the problem for me. One grabbed the microphone and began to sing, and the other grabbed a trumpet and began to play. Well, I guess you could call it that.

From that point on, things began to disintegrate. Whenever one of my boys slipped away for a quick dance or a quick beer—or even if he didn't—one of the guests would immediately offer to take over. I was absolutely baffled by this. I couldn't very well order my boys to stay put and refuse to budge—after all, these guests were also our sponsors! So I just stood where I was, waving my baton at a band which kept changing faces constantly. There came a time, late in the evening, when I gave a downbeat and didn't recognize a single person in my own band! What a night.

Everybody seemed to be having an absolutely wonderful time in spite of the fact that what we were playing didn't sound much like champagne music, but eventually the evening came to an end and everybody went home, including my boys, who were so extremely happy by then they went off without their instruments. Nobody was with me except for Bill Wilson, who was then doing our publicity. He and I looked at each other, looked at all the instruments strewn across the stage, sighed, and began carting them out to the band bus in the parking lot.

I was struggling across the floor, lugging my accordion under one arm and a bass drum under the other, when I encountered a lady slightly the worse for wear. She halted, focused on me with a little difficulty, and then said, incredulously: "You! I always thought you amounted to something. And here you are, just a— just a baggage carrier!" Saying which, she staggered off into the night, leaving me standing there with my big bass drum.

After that I made a firm decision never to mix champagne music with anything stronger than milk. Oh, maybe a little Geritol now and then. But no more beer.

6.

The Aldridges and the Otwells

If work and discipline are two requisites for success, then determination, or plain stick-to-itiveness, is another. And if I had to pick out anyone in the show to exemplify that quality, I'd hand the award to the little Aldridge sisters. Those two girls not only had a dream, but also enough determination to realize it. In fact, the number that got them on our show was "All You Have to Do Is Dream"—which has always seemed very appropriate to me.

I first heard them sing it in my office one morning, and they did such a beautiful job I rushed them down the corridor to the conference room where our production staff was having its regular meeting, burst in the door and cried, "Gentlemen! May I have your attention for just a moment, please? I want you to hear these two lovely ladies—Sheila and Sherry Aldridge!" I smiled and gestured at the girls, who gulped, swallowed, and—looking a little terrified—began to sing. When they finished, there wasn't a sound. Not a word. But the look on everyone's face showed that they were very pleased—even George Cates was smiling—so I said, "Well, gentlemen? What do you think?" Another pause, and then Jim Hobson, smiling broadly, said, "Lawrence, I think they're *great!*"

That coincided with my view exactly. Within a very short time we had invited the girls to appear as guest stars on our premiere show the following week, and the rest—as they say—is history.

But the Aldridge story isn't quite as easy as it sounds, because a great deal of planning, hoping, worrying, and dreaming had led up to that happy day.

I first met the girls in Nashville, Tennessee, in 1977, when the orchestra and I played there on our March concert tour. During the show I tiptoed out into the audience to greet some friends of mine sitting in the front row, and while I was chatting, I felt a gentle tug on the back of my coat. I turned around, and there were two young girls, both dressed exactly alike in white suits and both so pretty they looked like two little dolls. "Wow," I said, almost involuntarily, "how cute can you be?" Both started talking at once and told me they wanted to sing on our show. (I found out later they had already sent a tape in to our office. They had met Ken Delo and Gail Farrell, who were emceeing a March of Dimes telethon in Knoxville a few months earlier, and Ken had told them where to send a tape.)

But of course I didn't know that, so I told the girls to come backstage after the show and sing for me. They sang a song I had never heard before, but even so I could tell their voice quality was quite good. But as I explained to them, we already had a full roster of singers. Then I added that if they were ever in Los Angeles, they could check with me again.

Jon Williams, our polka-dancing star, with me in Pinkie's Cafe.

This surely looks like home to me! Macksville's main street reminds me of my hometown, North Dakota.

Tom Mareschal

Here are some of our talented trainees. Ava Barber has
built a huge fan following with her country music songs,
and has been coming up with hits on the record charts
also. She has been an absolute delight to have on the
show. So is her husband, Roger Sullivan, who has been a
great help to us, especially on
our road tours.

Tom Mareschal

Mary Lou Metzger and Jack Imel.
Mary Lou is one of the loveliest
ladies God ever put into this
world, and Jack one of the nicest
men. These two talented people
create their own dance routines,
and Jack assists in production of
our show as well as dancing and
playing marimba. Mary Lou can
do just about anything—sing,
dance, act, do comedy routines.
She never fails us.

I mentioned how versatile Mary Lou Metzger is, and on one show recently she not only sang and danced, she also drove a railroad engine across stage and wound things up by leading an elephant out in front of the cameras. (Here, she's just dancing with me.)

Tom Netherton, my North Dakota discovery. He's got it all—looks, talent, and youth. (And girls, he's still single.)

Lovely Anacani. This truly beautiful lady walked into me at Escondido just as I was walking out of our restaurant—walked back inside to audition for me—and then walked right into America's heart. Anacani learned so fast, and developed her talents so beautifully, she quickly became one of the most loved and most popular stars we've ever had. We feel so lucky to have found her.

I hired Kathie Sullivan because she has such a beautiful voice. Then she surprised all of us by coming up with a sensational flair for comedy and novelty numbers. Here she's singing "Doin' What Comes Naturally."

Gail Farrell. This lovely and talented lady developed from a chorus singer into a soloist, a pianist and arranger for our various vocal groups, and in the past couple of years has found herself in great demand for concert appearances. We're very proud of her.

Four of our excellent musicians: Violinist Joe Livoti, our concert-master; super saxophone-artist Russ Klein; Dixieland trombone virtuoso Bob Havens; and Henry Cuesta, the man with the golden clarinet. Perfection is a word that would apply to each one of these fine music men.

Russ Klein

Bob Havens

Henry Cuesta

Barney Liddell. Look at the smiles! I think both Barney and I are surprised he's been with us for 31 years. Barney is not only a fine musician, he's truly a wonderful friend. That's our excellent guitarist, Neil Levang, grinning in the background.

It was a lucky day for me when this lovely lady walked into my life. Doesn't she look like an angel? In the opinion of every one of us in the band, our Champagne Lady Norma Zimmer really IS an angel.

Leo North

In any musical show, you have to have a few fast-steppers, and we have three of the finest: Jack Imel, Arthur Duncan, and Bobby Burgess.

Our musical director, George Cates, is a brilliant man in many ways, and when it comes to music—he's a genius! George is fiercely dedicated to the betterment of the show and the band is much better today because of him.

I'm constantly amazed that anyone can be as full of creative ideas as our producer-director Jim Hobson is. Jim is solely responsible for getting the show on the air and keeping it moving and he does a superlative job. I consider him the finest director for a musical show in television.

Am I glad they didn't give up on me. Here are the Aldridge Sisters singing "All I Have to Do Is Dream," the song that won them a spot on our show. Sherry is on the left and Sheila on the right in this picture, which was taken during their first appearance on the show. (Neil Levang in background.)

And here it is: Proof positive that the boys have arrived.

The Aldridge Sisters and the Otwell Twins with "Dinah!"—their first guest appearance on national television after they joined us. That's Sheila, then Sherry on the left, and either Roger or David on the right; I just can't seem to tell them apart.

The Pittsburgh Steelers and I at the Mike Douglas Golf Tournament in Las Vegas, Nevada.

Dunlap-Turney
Photography,
Glendale, California

It would indeed be wonderful if every child could get the kind of love that this little girl receives from her parents, Guy and Ralna. Here is Miss Julie Miranda Hovis, with her beautiful mother. This is the picture Guy held up to the audience on tour, while he sang "You Light Up My Life."

Tom Mareschal

The reason Gail, Sandi, and Mary Lou are holding those animals in front of them, is because Sandi was then expecting. Over the years, we've become something of experts in camouflaging our expectant mamas.

And here's what Sandi was expecting—her brand-new baby daughter Emili, with Jenni, 9, Benji, 4, Ami, 7, and husband, Brent Griffiths. A wonderful, wonderful family.

Bobby Burgess—and partners: Far left, Cissy King, who added such grace and sparkle to our show for 12 years; left, Barbara Boylan, Bobby's first partner, who came out of retirement to help us for a few months; above, Elaine Niverson of Houston, Texas, Bobby's new partner, in her first appearance on our show.

Five of our lovely singing ladies, Gail Farrell, Sherry Aldridge, Sheila Aldridge, Kathie Sullivan, and Mary Lou Metzger. No wonder I don't want to give up my job.

Tom Mareschal

That was all they needed! No sooner had I gotten home from the tour than Julie Jobe stuck her head in my office door one morning and said, "There are two girls here who say they know you—the Aldridge sisters from Knoxville. Are you too busy to see them?"

"What?" I asked in astonishment. "They're here already? Well, okay, send them in."

They came in and sang another song I had never heard before— "Fernando." Again I told them they had potential but needed to work on their style and widen their repertoire and, of course, we still had no opening, not even for a guest spot. "I'm awfully sorry, girls," I said, "but we really have more singers now than we can handle." That dropped their faces way down, but again we promised to keep in touch with each other, and they flew back home to Knoxville and got jobs singing in two different clubs in the area. ("What we did," says Sherry, "was to go home and work long enough to earn enough money to pay for more airplane tickets to fly back to Los Angeles. For the next few months, we just about wore a track in the sky!")

A couple of months later, Julie stuck her head in the door with a "Guess who's here!" look on her face and said, "The Aldridge sisters are here again." "Okay," I laughed, "send them in."

Again they sang for me, and they had certainly improved. But again I was forced to tell them that there still wasn't a spot on the show. And again they flew back home to Knoxville, disappointed—but still determined.

Then in late July fate stepped in and took a hand. My daughter-in-law, Tanya, decided to go out on her own (in fact, she opened her act in my old stamping grounds, the famous Corn Palace in Mitchell, South

Dakota) and of course her departure left an opening for a guest spot. And would you believe that right after this happened, the Aldridge sisters flew back into my life for the third time? Well, they did! When Julie Jobe stuck her head in the door with that same "They're here again!" look, I surprised her completely by saying, "They are? Good! Wunnerful! Send them right in!" Julie looked so startled it was funny, but she ushered the two girls in immediately, and that's the morning they sang, "All I Have to Do Is Dream."

It was beautiful. Obviously they had been working very hard—every note was refined and pure, the harmony perfect, their rendition truly fine. They were most certainly good enough to present on the show and, with the production team's approval, that's exactly what we decided to do.

I remember taking the girls gently by the hand that memorable morning and saying, "Well, girls—how would you like to guest star on our opening show next week?"

Sheila gasped, and her eyes filled with tears (she's the younger and more emotional of the two). Sherry gasped, too, but managed to say, "Oh, Mr. Welk, do you really mean it?"

"I certainly do," I said. "With what you girls have been through, you deserve it!"

Both girls began crying then, but they were tears of joy. In fact, I can't remember seeing two people any happier—they acted like they were in heaven! "All our lives," said Sherry emotionally ... or was it Sheila? ... "all our lives we've dreamed about singing on your show! We've watched it with our parents ever since I can remember, and now—oh, it's a dream come true!"

The girls sang on our premiere show, which we taped in August of 1977, and we were literally flooded with approving fan mail afterwards. Nobody was happier about it than the girls and I, unless perhaps it was their parents—both girls are devoted to them. Their dad, Talton Aldridge, was a guitarist and singing star on radio during the thirties and forties ("Dad is the one who gave us our interest in music," say the girls) and their mother has always given her daughters the kind of total, unswerving faith and belief in them that made them believe they could move mountains.

I don't think the girls would mind if I shared a little story they told me about their mother. "After we had been on the show for a few months," they related, "we flew home for a short vacation. One morning mother brought out a package and handed it to us. And in it was the original audition tape we had mailed to the Welk office months before, along with a polite letter of rejection explaining that there were no openings on the show at that time. Mother had hidden it from us all those months, knowing it would have discouraged us completely if we had known about it. She had faith enough in us to let us make all those trips to Los Angeles in hopes of getting on the show! So we never lost hope, either."

As the girls said—that really is the kind of faith and determination that can move mountains.

I was very happy about finding the Aldridges of course. But by the time they made their first appearance on the show, I had gotten myself into something of a pickle because I had found *another* singing team which was very, very good—twenty-year-old twin boys, named Roger and David Otwell, from the little town of Tulia, Texas.

I had found the Otwells through a slightly more conventional route than the Aldridges. Their grandfather-in-law, Jack Love (that's as close as I can describe the relationship) is the father of the Otwell twins' sister's husband—follow me? At any rate, Mr. Love sent a tape and letter to our office, and Curt Ramsey and I were sufficiently impressed with it to put it in our "hot file" of possibilities. I had the boys in the back of my mind for several months because of their unusual voice quality and blend, and in September of 1977 I wrote and invited them to make a guest appearance on the show.

The boys told me later that pandemonium struck the day our letter arrived in the little town of Tulia, Texas, where they lived. "My girl friend's father works in the post office there," said David (or maybe it was Roger?) "and he recognized your picture on the outside of your letter. Everybody in the post office— well, everybody in the whole town knew you had written us before we did! And when we finally read your letter and found you were inviting us to guest on the show, well, Roger and I just about—well, we just couldn't believe it!"

But the Otwells had really been preparing for that letter all their lives. They had grown up in a musical family, and the two boys had sung together from the time they were very small, about six years old. "We sang everywhere," they told me, "in school, in our Church of Christ choir, at parties, the Lions Club. We were always waiting around for someone to ask us to sing." And they were always more than willing to perform for local charities, too.

"So when your letter came," marveled Roger—or was it David—"the whole town pitched in and raised three hundred dollars as a kind of farewell good-luck gift for us. The Lions Club gave one hundred, and the rest came from friends around town. Isn't that—wasn't that just *terrific!*" Both Roger and David looked absolutely dazzled as they told me about this and, looking into their fresh young faces, I realized how very nice they were themselves. I don't think I've ever in my life met a "nicer" pair of human beings than these two, and I would say every other person in the band agrees with me. I've yet to hear anyone make the slightest kind of criticism or unkind remark about the boys. They are just plain nice, the kind of sons every family would like to have. And they have one quality I just love—enthusiasm. They simply radiate it, it bounces off them like sun rays. To Roger and David, life is one big adventure, and they make everyone around them feel that way too. No wonder everybody likes them.

At any rate, the boys accepted the three hundred dollars their friends had raised, packed up their guitars, their hopes, their dreams (and a few relatives), and drove off to Los Angeles. I invited them to stay in our guest apartment at the Champagne Towers when they arrived, and then I brought them up to the house to visit with Fern and me for the evening. Next morning, I picked them up at eight o'clock and drove them to CBS for rehearsal, and that night they performed on the show.

Like the Aldridges, they were an immediate hit. They were so good I knew I wanted to hold on to

them, but I had no idea how to do it. We never hire
anyone new at the expense of someone old—never put
anyone out to pasture, so to speak, to make room for a
newcomer. Instead, we wait till there's a vacancy, or else
figure out some way to fit new people into our overall
picture. But now, with the Aldridges and Otwells, that
made *four* new singers, and I had no idea how to work
them in. We already had one highly popular singing
duo—Ralna and Guy; we had a trio—Sandi, Gail, and
Mary Lou, plus various other quartets and quintets we
put together from time to time. We really didn't need
two more singing duos.

So I didn't know what to do. I finally decided
to send all four youngsters to Escondido to work part
time while we tried to work something out. The girls
worked as singing hostesses and cashiers, and the boys
as singing busboys. Paul Ryan, manager of our Village
Inn Restaurant there, told me later that the boys were
absolutely sensational. "They'd show up right on the
dot," he said, "and start hustling dishes off the tables.
Then, one of the guests would tell me he was celebrating a birthday. I'd tell the boys, they'd tear off their
busboy jackets, grab their suit coats and guitars, sing
"Happy Birthday" with big, big smiles on their faces,
take off their suit coats, put their busboy coats back on,
and get right back to work!" Needless to say, Paul was
mightily impressed with the boys, and so was I. But
that still didn't solve our problem of getting all four of
them on the show.

For the next few weeks we invited first the
girls, and then the boys, or—if some of our artists were
out on tour—all four at the same time. But it was a
constant struggle till one day George Cates said
thoughtfully, "You know, Lawrence, those kids might
make a good quartet. I think their voices would blend."

I looked at him. "You might have something there, George," I said. "Let's try it."

The next time all four of them were scheduled for the show, I asked them to sing together for me. They hadn't sung more than four or five bars before we knew we had stumbled onto something absolutely terrific! Members of the same family often have exceptionally good blends, and with twins, I suppose it's even more so. And when we put those sisters and brothers together, the resulting close, warm blend sent chills up and down my spine! "Kids," I said excitedly, "when you go back to Escondido, will you do me a favor? Would you pick out a number you really like and go to work on it as a quartet? I think we might really have something. Would you do that?"

Four pairs of brown eyes looked at me. Four young faces regarded me soberly. No one said anything, but there was a definite air of—well, I guess you could call it hesitancy on their part. But after a moment, all four nodded and said yes they would try.

Next week they came into my dressing room and sang and again I felt gooseflesh crawling up my arms. As I've often said, the amount of goosebumps I produce is a pretty good indication of how much I like a number, and this one rated very, very high on my goosebump scale. "Kids," I said, "that's *good*, really good! Let me call George." George came in and listened to them and so did Bob Ballard, and we decided to use them on the show immediately.

Well if the viewers had liked them individually, they *loved* them as a quartet! There was something about those four fresh fine young people, singing together with such a close warm blend, that really got through to our listeners. But when I told the kids about the great reaction on the part of our fans, I was met with a very restrained reaction on their part. None of them said outright that they didn't want to sing together— they didn't have to—I could sense it quite strongly. And I could understand it too—they had been singing together as separate duos for a long time, they had confidence in their ability, they were comfortable in that slot. But together in a foursome, they were a little uneasy, a little unsure ("We were just plain scared," the boys admitted later.) And of course they hated to give up their dream of singing as two individual teams.

That became quite apparent when we were discussing what to call them. Several people in the band suggested "Brothers and Sisters," but Sheila demurred. "Oh, please," she said, "Sherry and I have worked so hard and we're so proud of our family name—couldn't we make it the Aldridges and the Otwells?" That seemed reasonable to me and that's what we did— currently their billing is the Aldridge Sisters and the Otwell Twins. That way, each retains their individuality, as well as their image as a quartet.

But if we had apparently successfully solved the problem of integrating all four youngsters into the show, I was still very much aware that the kids were not quite happy about it and were a little concerned over their new status. So one day I sat down with them and we talked the whole thing over—father to daughters, father to sons, friend to friend. I explained that when we first heard them sing together, we had not only discovered a brilliant new "sound," but also a way to give each of them a secure spot on the show. I tried to open their eyes to the positive things in their future— recording dates, personal appearances that would give them a chance to sing solos and duets, as well as group numbers; I pointed out that their potential as a quartet was infinitely more promising than as two separate singing teams. They listened gravely and intently, nodding occasionally, and by the time we parted, I felt we'd taken a big step forward.

All this happened in early spring. Then in June we went to Tahoe for our annual three-week engagement at Harrahs, and the first public appearance of the kids with our show. We decided to present them alone on one of our side stages (at Harrahs, there is a huge center stage, with two small stages on either side that look almost like shadow boxes). For the quartet, Jim Hobson came up with a lovely setting of trees and rolling hills, lighted as if by sunshine; and when the curtains parted, the audience saw Sheila and Sherry wearing ruffled green square-dance dresses, and the boys in modified dress-up cowboy clothes, looking so young, so healthy, and so attractive, they got a big round of applause before they sang a note. Sheila, who has a fine gift of gab, introduced each of them, and the twins grinned and informed the audience that "I'm Roger and I'm thirteen minutes older than David" (or maybe the other way 'round). Then they sang "Cotton Fields"—and the applause shook the room. They always had to sing an encore, and it seemed to me, after Tahoe, that four smiles got a little wider, and eight big brown eyes a little brighter. For the first time, they were beginning to understand their enormous potential as a quartet.

One morning back in Los Angeles, taping our new series of shows, there was a knock on my dressing-room door. It was the kids. "May we come in?" they wanted to know. "Certainly," I said, "what do you nice pests want now?" "Well," said Sheila, speaking as usual for the rest of them, "we've worked up a new song we thought you might like for the new show—and well, would you like to hear it?"

"I would," I said, giving them my full attention.

Roger struck a chord, and the kids looked at each other in a way that bespoke obvious closeness, genuine affection, plus hours and hours of working together, and they broke into "I'm Knee Deep In Love With You!"

For the third time since I'd met them, my goosebumps started acting up. The moment they finished, I grabbed them by the hands, cried "Come along with me, kids," and rushed them across the hall to Dinah Shore's dressing room. She's an old friend of mine—I play in her golf tournament every year at Palm Springs, and the boys and I entertain at the party following the tournament, and I've guested on her show so frequently she knows me pretty well. Even so, she was really startled when I flung open the door, cried "Hello, Dinah!" and then turned to the Aldridges and Otwells and said, "All right, kids, sing!"

Dinah was working on some embroidery when we burst in, and it fell back into her lap as she listened. Her eyes got bigger and bigger, and her smile got wider and wider, and the moment they sang the last note, she jumped to her feet and cried delightedly, "Lawrence, they've *got* to be on my show!"

A few weeks later they did sing on Dinah's show. I sat out in the audience, so pleased, so proud—I don't know who was more thrilled, Dinah, the kids, or I. For a group which had been singing together just a few short months, they had made absolutely sensational progress.

I think now, looking back, that the appearance on Dinah's show really did it for them. It was a major step that made them realize how much they could accomplish together. They had always worked hard and faithfully, but now they worked with an added sense of joy and real purpose.

And then came the capper. Less than a year to the day that the girls first sang with us, the foursome received an invitation to appear at Disney World in Florida—not just for a day or two but for a two-week feature engagement! Being invited to play Disney World was a sure sign they had arrived, and all of us in our Musical Family went around grinning from ear to ear.

I would say the Aldridges and the Otwells made it faster than anyone we've ever had on our show—and with very good reason, too, quite aside from their talent and good looks. First of all, they were willing to work—and work hard. They were willing to discipline themselves—and did. They had a dream and enough determination to stick to it (a quality the little Aldridges have to the nth degree). They were enthusiastic. And finally, each possessed the flexibility to adapt to changing circumstances and meet whatever new challenges came along. That's a mark of real maturity, real growth. And these four youngsters had it—not only the talent to meet new challenges, but the strength of character to meet them successfully.

I'm so very, very proud of them. I think they're a real gold feather in our cap. It took us a while to figure out a way to make them permanent members of the family. But we finally did.

POSTSCRIPT: You'll find a couple of postscripts throughout this book and I couldn't resist adding this one. When Roger and David went back to Tulia for a little vacation last April, they got a call from the Tulia Chamber of Commerce. "We couldn't imagine what it was," said the boys, "but we went down to their office and they drove us out to the edge of town. And there, just a few feet off the highway leading into town, they had erected a great big sign—must have been about four by eight feet—and do you know what it said?"

"No," I said. "What?"

"It said:

TULIA, TEXAS
HOMETOWN OF THE OTWELL TWINS

"Boys," I said, "you've really arrived!"

7.

Banaszak, Gerela, Oldham—and Welk

The Otwell twins' great enthusiasm not only endears them to everyone they meet, it lights up their own lives, too. I've always been very lucky in that respect myself. I get so enthusiastic about people or projects or a new show, I literally can't get to sleep at night—or wait to get going again in the morning, either! In fact, as the king in The King and I *used to say, I'm a real "puzzlement" to myself. Here I am at seventy-six, still so crazy about my work I send Sam Lutz and Don Fedderson to New York every spring to finalize arrangements with our sponsor for another new television season, even though I know before they leave that I'm committing myself to another year's hard work. But there's really nothing I'd rather do. I would much prefer to keep on bouncing out of bed at five every morning and spend the day working, than take off on the most luxurious vacation in the world. A vacation doesn't interest me. I'd rather work!*

And I've always thought I knew what enthusiasm was, too, till the day I met the Pittsburgh Steelers.
Wow. What enthusiasm! Those fellows nearly knocked
me out with their high spirits and will to win. I'm not
talking about a football game. I'm talking about a Pro-
Am golf tournament hosted by Mike Douglas in Las
Vegas, in the spring of 1979. Each foursome was made
up of professional football players, plus one show
business personality, and I don't think I've ever played
in any tournament anyplace where the level of enthusiasm was so high!

At seven o'clock that morning I was waiting
for the restaurant to open so I could get a bite to eat
before my scheduled tee-off time, when suddenly one of
the officials rushed up shouting, "Mr. Welk, the Pittsburgh Steelers have just hit off and Telly Savalas was
supposed to play with them, but he isn't here yet! Could
you fill in?" Could I! I grabbed my driver and in about
three seconds I was on the first tee, delighted to be
playing with the famous Steelers. And there in the flesh
stood three of their most famous players—John
Banaszak, Ray Oldham, and Roy Gerela—all beaming
and all extending a hand in welcome. They waited
quietly while I teed off, but when I sent a short drive
straight down middle of the fairway, they exploded with
enthusiasm. "Wonderful!" they cried (I wonder where
they got *that* word) "Wonderful! Listen, Mr. Welk, we are
gonna win this game, and you're gonna help us!" They
spoke with such positive enthusiasm, I believed it too.

But I was a little overwhelmed by them. They
were all so strong! They'd step up to the tee, muscles
rippling, and smash the ball two hundred and fifty or
even three hundred yards down the fairway. Then the
music man would step up and hit it about one hundred

and seventy. I felt like a weakling. But they didn't seem to mind. In fact, whenever any of us hit any kind of decent drive or sank a putt, the other three would pound us on the back, grab us in a bear hug, hop up and down with glee. Stuffy and pompous they were not.

We did quite well, too, till we came to a par 5. Then one of the fellows hit his second ball out of bounds. The next sent his ball into the lake. And the third landed in the sand trap. I got lucky and hit my ball straight down the fairway where it landed about one hundred and fifty-five yards from the green. When I got up to my ball, all three fellows were waiting for me. "It's up to you now, Lawrence," they said earnestly. "Gentlemen," I said, "don't worry about a thing. I've got everything under control." Then I pulled a five wood from my golf bag. "Oh, you don't want that, you want an iron," they advised, I hesitated but said, "Well, fellows, I believe I better stick with my wood here." I lined up my shot, took a swing, and sent the ball right up onto the green where it landed and rolled gently about six feet beyond the cup.

Well, you would have thought I landed on the moon! What compliments, what raves, what excitement! John and Ray and Roy each pumped my hand, pounded me on the back, and practically carried me up onto the green, where they insisted I be the one to try and make the putt.

"Okay," I said, "I'll try." I measured, took aim, said a little prayer, tapped the ball—and made the putt.

The Steelers went to pieces! They whooped and hollered, threw me in the air, tossed me around like a rubber ball. "Fellows!" I protested, "take it easy, I'm an old musician, treat me gently!" They paid no attention, just kept throwing me around. "We *told* you we were gonna win, Lawrence," they yelled, "we told you!" (I started out as "Mr. Welk." I ended up as "Lawrence.") And you know something? We *did* win— and we have the trophy and bruises to prove it.

After the eighteenth hole, as I was changing shoes in the locker room, Roy Gerela came rushing in and grabbed me by the arm. "Listen, Lawrence," he said rapidly, "they're interviewing us on national TV in the press tent. You've gotta be there too—you helped us win!" And he hustled me off to share in the glory.

Those were three of the nicest young men I've ever met in my life—skilled, controlled, dedicated, clean—there was not one word of profanity from any of them. They gave me a purely fun demonstration that day, of the power of enthusiasm and belief in yourself. Those Steelers just *knew* we were going to win. They concentrated on it, dedicated themselves to it, believed in it.

And we did win.

Enthusiasm made the difference.

8.

Our Family Grows

I'm often asked, "Where do you find your new people?" "What do you look for?" and "How do you train them?"

Well, we find them anywhere and everywhere. (I even auditioned one man, a whistler, in the men's room of a local ballroom, years ago.) That's probably my most unusual audition, but I never know when or where I'm going to find unexpected talent. For instance, I found Kathie Sullivan in the back seat of a limousine! Maybe I better explain that. I was on a personal appearance and book tour at the time, and Kathie was the local Miss Champagne Lady in Madison, Wisconsin, where we were scheduled to play a concert. (Lon Varnell, my tour manager, sometimes sets up contests in the cities where we play, and whoever wins meets with us and occasionally sings with our band on stage that night.) Well, Kathie won in the Madison area and, as is the custom in these contests, met Lon and me at the airport when we flew into town.

The three of us rode into Madison in a limousine which Lon had rented for the occasion. (I must tell you folks that Lon Varnell is the greatest tour manager who ever lived, and he takes care of me as if I were a baby.) Anyway, there we were, riding along in the limo, and I asked Kathie to sing a few bars of her favorite song for us. She sang "My Bill" in a voice so pure and so lovely, I hired her before she finished the song. I don't think I've ever hired anyone faster than Kathie. I just didn't want to lose that beautiful voice. In fact, I took her right along with me to the bookstore and had her sing for the fans. I asked her to sing "My Bill" so many times that day I just about drove her crazy. She finally groaned and said, "Please let me sing something else!" "Okay," I said. "Sing whatever you like. Just sing!"

Before I flew back to Los Angeles, I had talked her into coming out and singing on our show for the remainder of our season. She was then in her final quarter as a senior at the University of Wisconsin, so she was a little hesitant, but finally she agreed. Then, when our show went on hiatus the following March, she flew back to Madison and completed her studies, earning a Bachelor of Music degree.

I think Kathie has one of the loveliest voices I've ever heard, and when I hired her I envisioned her singing ballads and love songs and that type of thing. But one day, after she'd been with us a few months, Jim Hobson came to me and said, "Lawrence, did you know that Kathie Sullivan is a born clown? She can be really funny!" We talked it over and decided to see what she could do with a novelty song called "Second-Hand Rose." Kathie sang it with such charm, and the audience response was so positive, that she now does a comedy number for us every once in a while. I didn't know I was getting a comedienne when I hired her, but I guess I did!

Our talent comes to us in all kinds of ways. George Cates had worked with Norma Zimmer on occasional radio shows and he raved about her voice so much that I finally invited her for a guest appearance. One song and I fell in love with her voice, and beautiful personality too, and a couple of weeks later asked her— on camera—to be our Champagne Lady. (That may be the smartest move I ever made. She's still our Champagne Lady and her charm and loveliness have made that title peculiarly her own. Everybody loves Norma.) Then, let's see ... Joe Feeney was recommended to us by a priest; Ava Barber sent a tape and then followed me all around a golf course in Nashville, Tennessee, where I was competing in a tournament, while her husband, Roger, played tape recordings of her songs. Our new cellist Ernie Erhardt came to us highly recommended by other musicians. We auditioned one or two others, but after one session playing with our band, we knew Ernie was for us. Sandi came through a mammoth general audition at the old Palladium Ballroom in Hollywood, where she auditioned with her then-partner, Salli Flynn. Gail Farrell and Mary Lou Metzger both won College Bowl contests, which included a trip to Hollywood. Gail came to a dance at the Palladium that night, tagged in on me, and wound up singing on stage. Mary Lou simply telephoned to ask if she could sing for me. She could, she did, and she was hired.

Then there's Skeets Herfurt, our new saxophone man. I've had my eye on Skeets for a long time. In fact, about fifty years ago more or less, when my little band and I were booked into Eddie Ott's Broadmoor Club in Denver, Colorado, guess who was playing in the band just before us? Skeets Herfurt. Skeets has long been recognized as one of the great musicians of our day, so when Dave Edwards, our first saxophone man, decided to strike out on his own last spring, I knew immediately whom I wanted. I tracked Skeets down in La Jolla, California, and convinced him he should join us. A couple of weeks later, I invited him and his lovely wife, Dorothy, to spend a little time with me at our home in Palm Springs. This was a few days before the annual Pow Wow party at the Indian Wells Country Club, where my little jazz group and I entertain every year, usually on a Saturday night. The Pow Wow is always great fun, a wonderful party held outdoors under a full Palm Springs moon, with the soft and warm desert breezes blowing. In fact, last April I timed things so we played "When The Moon Comes Over the Mountain" just as the big, fat California moon began rising over the mountain range in the background. At times like that, when I'm playing music I love, with people I love, under a gorgeous sky blinking with stars, I know I'm in the greatest business in the world!

At any rate, Skeets was with me, and for a few nights beforehand, he and I entertained informally with the house band at the Country Club every night from about five to seven. And did I learn a lesson. I'd play my accordion, and quite a few folks would get up to dance. But when Skeets played, practically everybody in the place rushed out on the floor! He has one of the most irresistible dance beats I've ever heard in my life, and with the resurgence of interest in dancing in the past couple of years, Skeets is exactly what we need.

Speaking of dancing, brings me to our newest member, little Elaine Niverson, Bobby Burgess' new dancing partner. I didn't find Elaine. Bobby did. Or, to be more exact, one of Bobby's fans did. Bob spent hours interviewing and auditioning dozens of aspiring partners last spring, and he was getting a little discouraged too. Finally one of his fans, who was also a dancing teacher, suggested Elaine. One dance with her and Bobby knew his search was over. Elaine and her husband, Ray, also a dancer, had been operating one of the "Let's Dance" schools in Houston, Texas, but they moved to Long Beach, California, and opened a branch there, so Elaine could be on our show. (I might just tell you that Bobby added yet another member to our "family" that same spring, when he and his pretty wife, Kristie, became parents of a son, Robert Floren Burgess, who weighed in at nine pounds and two ounces on May 26, joining his big sister, Becki, who is two and a half. Kristie is Myron Floren's daughter, so it was an especially happy occasion for all of us.)

Our people come to us in all manner of ways, but I would say the great majority have been hired through the standard method of sending in tapes. Generally Curt Ramsey listens first, and if he hears any potential at all, he turns them over to me. I know, or at least I think I know, how hard it must be for some aspiring youngster to send in a tape and then wait around for weeks for an answer, so I try to answer as quickly as possible. But my schedule is so heavy that sometimes the tapes pile up, and it takes quite a while to listen to them all. We do the best we can.

I'm often asked what I look for in prospective members. Well, talent of course, a willingness to work hard and take direction, and that indefinable something called "charisma," a quality that grabs your attention and makes you want to know the person better. And as

I've said before, if a singer or musician can produce a good tone, I can add all the other ingredients necessary for success. Our makeup artists can make them look good; Rose Weiss performs magic with her costumes; our musical arrangers bring out their best points. But if the voice, the quality, isn't there—there's little I can do.

But if it is there ... aaaaah! ... that's what this book is all about. Then we train and develop our newcomers in ways which I feel would benefit the whole nation. If enough qualified businesspeople would do the same type of thing for young people interested in *their* particular field—teach them the tricks and skills of the trade and inculcate them with the basic fundamentals of wholesome living, what a boost that would be for this country. What a boon for the youngsters. And what a boon for the employer! I cannot emphasize strongly enough the deep and satisfying joy, the great enrichment that comes into the life of any employer who takes the time and trouble to work with young people. It adds a dimension of joy into your life that comes no other way.

And you don't have to be a genius to do it. Look at me if you need any encouragement. I've had less schooling than any of the poeple I've trained. On the other hand, I have qualities that most successful businesspeople have—a know-how and knowledge that go along with the job, an ability to understand and relate to human nature, and enough experience in life to be able to pass on the advice and information that can help the most.

I never really realized that I had developed any kind of technique or specific knowledge to use in training our people until I began writing my books.

Then, trying to explain it to Bernice, I realized that almost without knowing it I had developed a certain technique. I call it "The Carrot System." (Remember the old fable about the donkey who flatly refused to budge, even though his master beat him repeatedly? Finally the frustrated master dangled a carrot on the end of a stick in front of the donkey's nose and the donkey took off like a jackrabbit.) Well that same technique works with us stubborn humans just as well as it does with donkeys. Force rarely accomplishes what you desire. But setting up a desirable goal—"dangling a carrot"—does!

So that's the first thing we do in training our new people—set their goals high, aim at the stars, set a goal so dazzling that they will work as hard as possible to attain it.

Then after the goal is set, we use encouragement. I try never to discourage, always to encourage, and to use compliments whenever possible. In the beginning I didn't do that. Possibly as a result of my own early training. I felt that too much approval might "spoil" people. I felt that if I didn't point out their faults, they would automatically know I was proud of them. But one day Gordon Malie, an exceptionally fine man, a drummer in my first little band in Yankton, came to me after a sensational solo and said, "Lawrence, what do I have to do to get a compliment out of you?" I was startled at the obvious unhappiness and disappointment in his voice. I'd been telling everybody else what a fine performer I thought he was—I just hadn't told him! And I realized for the first time how much a word of honest praise could mean. From that time on I made a point of complimenting people whenever possible. I discovered it not only makes them happier for the moment, it spurs them on to even higher accomplishments.

I might add that when I do have to correct or discipline anyone, I do it as kindly and gently as possible. And I always do it in the privacy of my office or dressing room, never in front of someone else, as a mark of my respect for the dignity of the individual.

Most of all, I show interest in them—great interest—and for me that's easy, because I really *am* interested! I love it when they learn new songs on their own, or come in with new ideas, or tell me they're taking lessons. I have such great respect for Gail Farrell along this line. She came to us with little more than a fresh prettiness, a pleasant voice, a degree in music, and overwhelming ambition. Today, simply by working on herself, she has developed a voice so beautiful she sings many of the obligatos in our choral arrangements with the band, plays piano solos, and does occasional musical arrangements for us. You've perhaps noticed the arrangements she has done in this past year for the Otwells and Aldridges. Gail has unleashed a whole new sound for the kids, and her potential as an arranger and performer in this business is simply tremendous. I foresee a great future for her—and it all started with a little girl who came to us fresh out of school, totally inexperienced, but determined to make something out of her life.

I'm completely sold on our people from the time I find and hire them. And once I'm sold on them, I keep selling them all the time—to themselves as well as everybody else, and this brings great, great, joy to me. I let them know from the start that I like them, that I'm interested in them—I phone them, invite them in for chats, share jokes with them. And I'm a great one for shaking hands or giving a quick hug—and I was doing this long before psychiatrists came along and told us how necessary it was. It all helps build the warm and close "family feeling" which is the undergirding of our system. If I had to pick out one facet of our life style which is more important than any of the others, it would certainly be this family feeling.

And it comes very easily to an employer to think of himself as a "parent," and the employees as his "children." Any good parent does everything possible to enhance the lives of his children. Any good child does what he can to please his parents. In a nutshell—that's the essence of our system.

We show our family concern in many, many ways. For example, one of the basic rules of our organization (in the orchestra, that is) is that every member must go on every road tour. Our fans deserve the best we can give them, and when we promise to be there in person, we do everything we can to fulfill that promise.

But there are exceptions. One time while we were on tour, Ralna's sister, Jane, fell desperately ill back home in Los Angeles. Without question, we allowed Ralna to fly home to be with her while she was so critically ill. Then again, a couple of years ago, Ralna and Guy finally added to their family the child they had been longing for—and you never saw such delighted parents! Little Julie Miranda is a beauty, I have to admit, and I think all of us in the Musical Family were as thrilled and ecstatic as her new parents. All the girls got together and gave a mammoth shower for Ralna—and Guy, too, as it turned out. The whole band—husbands and wives, some one-hundred strong, jam-packed into Mary Lou and Richard Maloof's home for a giant-size shower; and the fellows "oohed and aahed" right along with the girls every time Ralna opened another package.

I realized how close Ralna and Guy were to their baby, and yet I was really taken aback when the two of them came up to my house one night and asked that I excuse Ralna from the upcoming March tour. "But folks," I objected, "you know we all have to go on tour. Our fans expect it."

"I know," said Ralna, sitting on the sofa in a white sweater and skirt and looking a little like a madonna as she spoke, "I know, Lawrence, but I just can't leave Julie for ten days. Not while she's this young."

I sat silently for a moment and then Guy spoke up and said, "We just can't *both* of us leave that little girl for ten days! And we can't take her along either, it would be too hard on her. Maybe if I went out on stage and explained it to the folks—they would understand."

I thought about it. "Could you sing your songs with someone else?" I asked him.

Guy considered. "Gail could do it," he said finally.

I looked at these two youngsters who had played such a great part in our success—two young people who had waited almost ten years for their baby—and I decided that probably folks *would* understand the depth of Ralna's love for their child. I knew how much it meant to them. And so I agreed to Guy's going alone on that particular tour. Well as it turned out, Guy's idea was a sensation. He came out on stage with a huge photo of Ralna and the baby—the picture must have been about eight by ten feet—and told the folks exactly why Ralna was staying at home. Every mother in the audience could readily understand it. Then Guy held up the picture, turning slowly around and around so that everyone in the arena could see it—and sang, "You Light Up My Life." The audience just loved it.

Rules are made to be broken of course. There are always exceptions. And I felt that Ralna and Guy had a strong enough case to warrant an exception. I think this also exemplifies the kind of "family feeling" I'm talking about. In that instance, I did not look at Ralna and Guy as "employees" who sang on the show. I looked on them as my "children," and did what I thought was best for them.

Any employer who does the same thing will find a warm, close supportive family feeling growing in his organization. And if my experience is any criterion, he will also find that it adds immeasurably to his success and happiness as a businessman, an employer, and a human being.

9.

Freedom in the Family

Of course, as in any family—we lose some. That's only natural, that happens in any family. Children grow up, want to try their wings, get out on their own. That's part of life, and because we operate in total freedom, I wouldn't have it any other way. But, of course, when "children" leave it's painful.

And whenever it happens we are inundated with telephone calls and letters from our fans, wanting to know why so and so has left. I can sympathize with their interest, in fact, I'm grateful for it, and in many cases I'm tempted to talk about it. But I have never talked about the reasons why people leave us, mainly because I don't want to hurt them in any way, or jeopardize their professional future. They may be off our show, but they're certainly not out of my heart, and I wish only the best for anyone who has ever been part of our Musical Family.

Performers leave for a variety of reasons. I'll not comment on any of them, but obviously whenever someone leaves, there's a reason for it. Perhaps our relationship has eroded, perhaps they want to move on to another phase of show business, perhaps they weren't able to live up to our rules and regulations.

I might just say a word about that. I don't believe in a lot of rules, that's true—freedom is my whole belief. But any organization requires a few ground rules, and we do too. Ours are very few in number, but they are strictly enforced. All our members are required to attend every rehearsal, for example, to attend that rehearsal on time, to know their songs or music thoroughly by show time, and to go on every tour with us, unless specifically excused for some unusual reason. That's about the extent of our requirements, but as I said, they are strictly enforced. We just couldn't operate a big orchestra like ours if people showed up late for rehearsals or shows. One person, being only a few minutes late, could hold up an entire company, and union laws require that the whole company be paid in full for the time a rehearsal is scheduled. So tardiness, failure to learn songs, or absence from rehearsal are things we just can't tolerate. We may go along for years trying to help someone overcome his faults and learn to live up to the rules (and we have!) but sometimes we are forced to bow to the reality of a situation and simply release a performer who cannot, for one reason or another, learn to abide by the rules. That's unhappy for all of us. I've often said we feel worse than our fans do whenever we are parted from one of our "family," no matter what the reason.

Occasionally during the twenty-four years we've been on national TV, a performer has felt impelled to move out on his own, and try to become a star in his own right. Of course that's their privilege,

and I accept it completely. I sometimes talk with them
and point out the security and opportunity they may be
forfeiting if they leave, but I would never pressure
anyone into staying. Freedom is the watchword of our
organization and not just a pretty word that sounds nice
when we say it. Freedom *is* the key word. There's no
pressure, no demands, no forcing in our system. Our
people know we'll encourage them, help them, open up
opportunities, maybe even give them a little push if they
need it. But never, ever, will we force or order them.
And never do we tie them up legally. I just don't believe
in it.

No one in our organization is signed to a
contract, and in show business that's a rarity. I realize
contracts are not used in the normal course of most
businesses, except perhaps at the executive level of
management. But in show business, signing contracts is
a way of life, the idea being that no producer or
producing company wants to nurture and develop a star
and then have the star take off when he becomes popular
and famous.

Well I don't like that either! It's happened to
me on occasion, and I can't say it made me jump for joy.
But I still wouldn't tie anyone up with a contract,
because to me, freedom is too precious. I think we work
best in freedom; we develop our talents best. In our
profession, what we're selling is music ... entertainment ... happiness. And how can you be happy
without freedom?

No, I much prefer an open, relaxed situation
where you can talk things over on a personal basis
without agents or lawyers getting involved, where you
can sit down and talk heart-to-heart. If both sides are
fair and right-minded, you can almost always get

problem spots ironed out. That's the way we've operated for over fifty years in the band and—it works. In spite of the fact that a small percentage of people have left us over the years, the overwhelming majority have stayed with us longer than any other orchestra in the history of the music business—something that means a great deal to me. Barney Liddell has been with us the longest, which is rather a surprise considering what he said to me when I first hired him. That was back in 1948, when we were playing at the Trianon in Chicago. Barney had been playing trombone with the Elliot Lawrence Band, a somewhat "swingier" organization than ours. And the first thing Barney said to me after he joined us was, "Mr. Welk, I appreciate the job and all that, but I don't know if I'll be able to stand playing your type of music for very long." Well, so far Barney has stood it for thirty-one years. But he's not the only long-term member. Myron Floren, Dick Dale, Larry Hooper, Curt Ramsey, and Jimmy Roberts have all been with us for thirty years; Kenny Trimble for twenty-two. (And in all those twenty-two years, Kenny has never missed a show, never been late, and never done anything else wrong, as far as I can tell, and I'm a pretty good watchdog!) About half the orchestra personnel has been with me for many, many years, and in the music business that's rare. The only way I can explain this extraordinary loyalty is because we operate in complete freedom.

I've never asked Myron to sign a contract. I've never asked any of our people to promise faithfully they'll never leave. Instead, I let them know that as long as they do the best job of which they're capable, they have a lifetime job with me. I want them to understand that I value them so much I will do everything I can to make it worth their time and talent to stay with me. I want what's best for *them*, because I learned long, long ago that if it's good for them, it's probably good for the band.

To me, that's a far more powerful concept than signing contracts. And somehow, knowing you can leave often makes you want to stay! That's old human nature at work. We all want what we can't have.

My ideas about freedom also include freedom to work at other jobs if you want to and have the time. It's called moonlighting. Our people are always going out on personal appearances on their own, and it seems to me they always come back an improved version of themselves. That's one reason I encourage it! Our situation is a little different, I'll admit. We don't need or demand a full five-day workweek; so as long as our people do their work with us at the top of their ability, that's all I ask. If they have extra time or energy and want to work another job—why not? Chances are their new skills will add to their performance on both jobs. I would never put a roadblock in the path of anyone's chance to grow.

So that's why I don't feel as bad as I might when people leave us. It's their choice, their right, their decision. It's an expression of our total commitment to the concept of freedom. And I believe it keeps our level of performance higher and makes us value and appreciate one another all the more.

POSTSCRIPT: I thought you might be interested in knowing how I arrived at my strong feelings about freedom, as exemplified by "no contracts." I think it really started back on the farm where a verbal promise or a handshake was fully as binding as a legal written contract. Once the people in our little village had given their word, there was no way they would go back on it. That feeling was ingrained into me as far back as I can remember.

And then when I was in my late twenties, I had an experience which really crystallized my feelings about contracts. It happened in 1931, when one of the biggest musical agencies in the nation signed me to a contract which was to be valid till they earned a million dollars in commissions. And if they earned a million, just think what the boys and I would earn! I was so thrilled by this turn of events I wrote home imme-diately, and the next week the Emmons County Record came out with a front-page picture and story: HOME TOWN BOY MAKES GOOD. GETS MILLION-DOLLAR CONTRACT! I felt we had really arrived, and was flying so high I had trouble touching the ground. But then reality began to inch in. Week after week went by—and no jobs. I'd call the agency every day and they'd say, "Sorry, we're having trouble selling you, Mr. Welk. Nothing so far." After a few more weeks of this, they stopped taking my calls altogether.

I was desperate. Here we were, with a million-dollar contract and everybody thought we were rolling in dough, when the truth was we weren't even working! It got to the point where we were getting downright hungry, so finally I did what I'd been doing before the contract—went out and booked the band myself. The only difference was that now I had to pay the agency a twenty-percent commission! And as tight as I am, that didn't sit too well.

The trouble was, of course, that we were just one of a hundred bands the agency represented. At the top were Guy Lombardo, Jan Garber, Paul Whiteman, Hal Kemp, bands of that caliber—and Welk and his little Hotsy Totsy band were so far down the list the agency had trouble remembering our name. I could understand that, but it still didn't help us eat or keep a roof over our heads!

I finally managed to book the boys and myself into a summer job at Twin Lakes, Wisconsin. It paid three hundred dollars per week, which sounded pretty good, but after paying union fees and agency commissions, it left only a few dollars apiece for the eight of us—not very much, especially for a man with a brand new wife. (Fern and I had been married only a few months. Looking back, I wonder how she ever stuck with me!) Anyway, things were so difficult for us that I finally decided to ask for a release from our contract. It seemed to me we had been doing much better before we signed it.

But as usual I couldn't get through to the agency on the phone. I'd call every day. They wouldn't take my calls. I'd drive the sixty miles to their Chicago office and wait all day for someone to see me. Nobody ever did. I didn't know what to do till finally the telephone operators, who worked next door to the dance pavilion at Twin Lakes, came up with an idea. They knew us pretty well from dancing with us every night, so they were our pals. They called the agency every five minutes and managed to tie up their lines so completely that one of the officials finally broke down and agreed to see me.

Next day I drove in to see him, explained our predicament, and asked for a release. "You haven't been able to book us," I told him, "and I've got these seven men depending on me to find them jobs. If you'll release us, I promise we'll come back to you when we've built up more of a name for ourselves, so you can book us easier."

"Oh," said the agent, "I don't see how we can do that. We've got an airtight contract with you."

"But it's just not right to tie us up this way and then not find any work for us," I cried in frustration. "It's ... it's just not the American way!"

Well, I don't know if it was my appeal to his Americanism or his conviction that he'd never be able to sell the Hotsy Totsy Boys anywhere, but eventually he arranged for a release. (And true to my promise, we returned a few years later when our name was bigger, and worked very amicably for several years.)

That experience certainly shook my faith in contracts. Far from guaranteeing us a wonderful future, it had just about put the finishing touches on it. But it also opened my eyes anew to the power of doing things on your own. Forced to keep on booking the band myself, I learned things out on the road that are still standing us in good stead today.

So my first severe brush with contracts put a scare into me, and I've never felt the need for them. My agent-manager, Sam Lutz, and I had a handshake deal back in 1945. We're still together. Don Fedderson and I agreed to work together in 1955. He's still in charge of our syndicated production. Not one of our people is under contract to me. We stay together because we *want* to stay together.

My primary goal in dealing with anyone who works with me is not to tie them up in a contract, but to do what's best for *them*—to open doors for them, to help them in any way I can to explore their potential. If that door sometimes leads away from me—well, that's part of life. For a while—we've helped each other grow. We've maintained our "freedom in the family." And that's the most important thing of all.

Freedom.

Part Three

Our Business Family

10.

The Ted Lennon Story

I first met Ted Lennon in October of 1957. I was deeply involved with a second television show at the time ("Top Tunes and New Talent") and it was giving me a little trouble, because we just couldn't find enough youthful talent good enough to use on the show. I was shocked and disturbed to discover how few young people were really prepared, and now as I look back, I realize this was another incident that shaped my mind about the importance of training for young folks. Lots of them had raw talent, but it hadn't been refined, and was in no shape to be presented as "entertainment."

I was getting desperate in spite of the tons of audition tapes and records that were being mailed in to us, and I finally concluded that what I needed was a talent scout to go out on the road and track down some really good young performers for the show.

I first asked Bill Lennon, father of the Lennon Sisters, if he would do it, but he was so busy with the girls he couldn't take the time. "But I think my brother

Ted would be wonderful," he said. "He's had experience in show business, he can make good judgments,
he's a hard worker, he's a family man ... " he went on
and on, outlining Ted's abilities. "Okay," I said, "let me
talk with him."

　　As it happened, the orchestra and I were out
on a short tour and returned to the studio on the day of
my appointment with Ted. He said later that he was
vastly impressed to learn that we had come home from a
tour only that morning and would be working all day to
present our television show that night. To me, however,
it was just part of the game, and after a short hour's nap
to refresh myself, I went out to meet Ted. He turned
out to be a tall and personable young man in his early
thirties, with hazel eyes, brown hair, and a quick Irish
grin. We chatted for a while and I outlined what I
wanted. Ted hesitated. "Well," he said, "I don't know if
Bill told you, but I have a wife and seven children, and
I'm devoted to them. I really don't think I could travel
and be away from home too long."

　　I liked that. And I said, "Well, you have my
word that you'll never have to be on the road any longer
than two weeks at a time." (Ted told me later that *he*
liked *that*!) I was sufficiently impressed with him to
make a tentative agreement, a handshake agreement, as
I've done all my life. "Let's try it," I said. "If you don't
like the job or feel things are not quite right, you're free
to leave at any time, no questions asked. And I'll retain
the same privilege."

　　Ted agreed. At the time he was selling beer to
retailers, managing an apartment house, and doing
anything else he could manage to squeeze in. When you
have seven children, it keeps you hustling! I told Ted to
give his current employer two weeks' notice, because I

felt it wasn't fair for him to leave immediately, so he set to work winding up his jobs and getting ready to "talent-scout."

As I say, that was in October. By Christmas I had raised his salary and given him a cash bonus. What a job he did for us. Every day he mailed us a report—whom he had seen, what his evaluations were, and so on and so forth. He used to write to college campuses and little theaters and radio and television stations beforehand to have the talent lined up and waiting when he arrived. He must have auditioned literally hundreds of singers and dancers. Even so, he found little usable talent, which only underscored my feelings about allowing youngsters to get the training they need.

Eventually the lack of talent forced us to give up the show. But I didn't want to give Ted up, because I felt he was far too good to lose. So I kept him on as a kind of talent coordinator, booking our talent and keeping an eye out for more. And also, I had a feeling—call it instinct—that this young Irishman had a lot on the ball. So I introduced him to my business manager Ed Spaulding, who had been doing a superb job of handling our business affairs. "See if this Ted Lennon can't help you, Ed," I suggested.

Ed took him under his wing. We were then involved in our first big expansion—constructing the Lawrence Welk-Union Bank Building at 24th and Wilshire in Santa Monica, in which we would have a top-floor suite. I won't go into the ramifications of the deal because I'm no businessman—I just know how to hire good ones! But I do remember it was the first new office building built in Santa Monica in over thirty-eight years and was a source of great interest to the city fathers. We had barely gotten into the project, however, before my good and dear friend Ed fell very ill. So Ted suddenly found himself up to his ears in a multimillion-dollar project with not a whole lot of experience to protect him—or us!

It didn't stop him. He plunged right in, studying everything relating to the project, spending hours conferring with Ed, and poring over books that would help him. He stayed a jump or two ahead of the game all along and the whole thing came off beautifully.

I was impressed. Obviously he knew how to recognize an opportunity and take advantage of it and I was impressed by that. He was a hard worker who came in earlier and stayed later than anyone else and I was impressed by *that*. But there was more to Ted, and I think it was his—well, call it his moral soundness that got through to me. He was one of eight children. In fact, he was the sixth, as I myself was, which makes some kind of bond between us. He had had a warm and loving family life, but when he was only ten his father died, and what had been routine chores and working for pocket money, suddenly became an integrated effort on the part of all seven Lennon boys to help support the family. They worked as box boys, butchers, painters, deliverymen—anything they could find. Later they formed a quartet and began earning money that way, too. And all of them took their money home to their widowed mother, whose own moral and religious training had been thoroughly instilled into each of them. "She wasn't very big," says Ted, now, "but she was powerful! And she was beautiful, too—she looked very much like our Kathy Lennon of today." All seven boys were devoted to their mother and never questioned turning over their money to her. They were a family together, the money was needed, they would all share.

It was a lesson in honesty and compassion which shows in Ted's exemplary behavior today.

But I'm getting ahead of my story. I wanted to point out how Ted has made an enormous success of his life in spite of the fact that he had only a minimum education by today's standards—high school only, with no college or special education of any kind.

But he had the best education of all—life and experience! He worked constantly all through his earliest years—learning, growing, looking for ways to move up. And he certainly moved straight up, from the day he went to work for us! From talent scout to talent coordinator, from part-time assistant to Ed Spaulding to full assistant; and then, when Ed passed on, to complete direction of all the business activities of our corporation.

Along the way he did everything he could to further his growth—and ours. He joined the Chamber of Commerce, boned up on business law and possible new investments. He would come to me, bursting with enthusiasm over some new idea—and sometimes I thought it was pretty far out and wouldn't act on it. But I loved his zest, his constant searching, his eagerness to make something out of his life.

He helped us find Escondido and is in full charge of our expansion there today. He masterminded and helped develop the Lawrence Welk Plaza, overlooking the Pacific Ocean in Santa Monica. He has his finger on the pulse of every facet of our operations and is the one man on whom I rely with the utmost confidence, truly my right-hand man in every sense of the term. And today he is the executive vice-president of our corporation.

From the day we met, he grew and *we* grew. (And his family grew! Ted and Peggy, his pretty blonde wife, have thirteen children and twenty-three grand-children at last count!)

And when I see Ted today, standing up in a meeting filled with high-powered business executives, and listen to him talk with confidence and incisive knowledge, outlining a plan of action that makes won-derful sense—I am so full of pride I can hardly stand it! I think back to the days when he was struggling to support his young family, first as a beer salesman, and then as a talent scout, and I realize what a long, long way he has come. I've mentioned before the great joy I feel when one of our young performers makes it on our show. But it's no more than the pride and satisfaction I feel when I see someone like Ted come into his own.

I've gone into considerable detail with Ted's story, even though he is someone you don't really know too well except perhaps as an uncle of the Lennon Sisters, because I wanted to show that the system which works so well in our rather glamorous show-business life, works equally well in ordinary business life.

Just like our musical trainees, Ted, too, learned "on the job." Like them, he thrived in an atmosphere in which we opened up opportunities and future goals (and he was always quick to grasp for "the carrot" and prove his talents)! Like them he was highly motivated by the knowledge that he would share in the profits he helped to earn.

Ted, today, would be a tremendous asset to any major business in the country—and I know it. He could leave me at any time if he chose—and I know that, too. But it doesn't worry me any more than the knowledge that any of the stars on our television show could do the same thing. Because I know that what holds us together is far more binding than any kind of legal contract. Freedom.

Freedom holds us together, because we want to stay together, because we know that working together in mutual support can take us further than working separately. We have learned that helping each other achieve a mutual goal unleashes unsuspected talents and enriches life for all of us. And, paradoxically, knowing we can walk away at any time seems to weld a closeness and loyalty that cannot be forged any other way, "Freedom of Action" has become one of the basic operating principles of our system. Ted Lennon exemplifies to the fullest how this principle helps people reach the very height of their potential. I would say that Ted has utilized a very, very high degree of his inborn talents through our system and there is really no limit to his future.

Our system works as well with the waitresses and busboys at Escondido as it does with the singers and dancers on our show. And it works just fine for a talent scout, and an ex-farmer from North Dakota, too.

11.

A Dream Come True

When Ted walked into my office and handed me the plans and mock-up for the building which would complete the entire Lawrence Welk Plaza in 1979, I couldn't help remembering how this whole beautiful thing got started—and what happened to me the day I applied for my first real-estate loan in Santa Monica.

That was back in the mid fifties, shortly after we had opened at the old Aragon Ballroom on Lick Pier in Ocean Park. I have played in a few run-down places in my time, but this one was really suffering! But I didn't care. I was happy to play any place, as long as the boys and I could keep on eating.

We had no sooner opened, however, than the miracle of television touched us and changed our lives forever. Television brought the boys and me the success we had been dreaming about for more than thirty years, and for the first time in our history, we not only began eating regularly, we also began making some pretty good money. (And, for the first time in a long time, the Aragon spruced up and got a new lease on life, too.)

The orchestra did so well I even began dreaming about building us a little office building. We certainly needed one. Our first office in Santa Monica was one room at the William Tell Motel. The next was a storefront building on Santa Monica Boulevard. It opened right onto the street, and as we became better known through television, people would walk right in to look us over. I'll never forget the day three little boys came in. When they saw me sitting at a desk piled high with mail, sheet music and record albums, their eyes widened. "Gee, Mr. Welk," said one of the youngsters, "do you have to work?" "Oh, surely," I said. "Every day." "Gosh," said the little fellow, looking disappointed, "I thought you were rich!" "Well," I said, "if you want to succeed, you have to keep working." (I was trying to get my message across even in those years.)

I wasn't rich but I did think that maybe I could manage a little office building of some kind. I began looking for lots on Sunset Boulevard, close to the famous Ciro's nightclub—that seemed like the height of glamor to me. But my business advisor, Ed Spaulding, talked me out of it. "Lawrence," he said, "don't do it. Sunset Boulevard is on the way down. Wilshire is on the way up." I had always considered Ed a brilliant businessman, and that piece of advice turned out to be a tremendous boon to this accordion player.

With Ed's advice in mind, I kept my eyes open for a possible lot on Wilshire, and one day I found what seemed to me the perfect location, a lot 40 by 150 feet, right across the street from a beautiful little park at 24th and Wilshire. The park was lovely, with lots of trees and a pond and flower beds. I thought how nice it would be to build a two-story building where you could look out and see all that beauty. I've always loved open spaces and trees and sunshine, and even though that lot cost more than I could afford to pay, I just couldn't get it out of my mind. So one day when I was making my regular weekly deposit in the bank where we had dealt since we had arrived in Santa Monica, I got up enough nerve to ask about a loan. I went up to one of the loan officers, told him about the lot, its location, and why I thought it would be a good investment. "And I was wondering," I said, "how much money you folks could lend me?"

He regarded me without expression for a few moments. Then he said, "Mr. Welk, I'll have to discuss this with the other officials." He disappeared into another room. A couple of minutes later he was back. "I'm sorry, Mr. Welk," he said, "but I'm afraid I have bad news. We won't be able to lend you anything."

"Nothing at all?" I asked.

"Nothing at all," he said flatly.

Naturally I was terribly disappointed, but not really surprised. I had already learned that musicians don't have the best credit rating in the world. I guess that goes for show business in general. I accepted the whole incident philosophically and put it out of my mind. But not the lot!

A couple of weeks later a man named Stan Zundell phoned me and identified himself as manager of a new bank opening at 15th and Wilshire, and asked if I would be kind enough to cut the ribbon at the opening festivities. That was something new. I felt I was finally getting places, and happily agreed. It turned out that Mr. Zundell was a musician too. He had played alto sax to earn his way through school. We struck up quite a rapport, and in no time he had asked me if I would be

willing to move part of our account to his bank. I
thought about it. His bank was much closer to our
office, which made it more convenient, and we had
become almost instant friends. I decided to make the
move.

Not long afterwards the first bank called and
expressed regrets at my leaving. "Couldn't you leave
part of your account with us, Mr. Welk?" they asked.
"Oh," I said, "this new bank is more convenient, and
Mr. Zundell and I are pretty good friends. I think I'll
leave things as they are." There was a pause, and then
my caller said, "Mr. Welk, you might be interested to
know that the man who turned down your loan applica-
tion is no longer with us."

So finally, we were able to buy my dream lot.
That was not only my first step into real estate, it was
also the beginning of our Lawrence Welk Plaza of today.

The next step was the unlikely one of a lunch
date with a horse fancier named Bert Martin, a well-
known racing-stable owner. I had met him through a
mutual friend of ours, George Thomas, who also had a
great interest in racing. Not too long after that, as I
recall, Mr. Martin invited Ed Spaulding and me to
lunch. I knew—or I thought I knew—what he had in
mind, and on the way out to his ranch I said to Ed,
"Now Ed, whatever you do, don't let me get in the
horse business!"

But Bert Martin was not only a man for whom
I had the highest respect, he was also a super salesman.
We chatted for a while. I told him how well our
orchestra was doing and about my lot in Santa Monica
and my dream of building a two-story office building.
He, in turn, pointed out that my investing in his horse
farm would be a very good thing for me, and the many

reasons why such a move would make good sense for our expanding orchestra business. "And besides," he added, "think how much your children would love it!" That really got to me. Our daughter Donna is a horse lover from way back, and has always managed to have a horse to ride. I began to waver and finally said, "But Bert, even if I wanted to, I couldn't join you. We don't have that kind of finances, do we Ed?" I looked appealingly at Ed. To my astonishment he pursed his lips and said "Oh, I think we could move things around so we could manage it." I burst out laughing, jumped to my feet, walked across the room, grabbed Bert's hand and said, "Okay Bert—we're partners!"

He grinned too but didn't say a word. Instead, he reached over, picked up the phone, and called Harry Volk of the Union Bank in downtown Los Angeles. "Harry," he said, after the usual amenities, "do you know Lawrence Welk?" (I couldn't help overhearing him, and my ears were really perked up.) "Oh, you know his television show? And you like it? (That sounded good.) "Well," he went on, "Welk wants to build a two-story office building in Santa Monica. He's got a fine location right across the street from a beautiful little park at 24th and Wilshire, and I thought maybe it would be a good spot for a branch office for you. Sounds promising? Good! I'll send Welk down to talk with you."

That phone call was what propelled me into my first real-estate venture—actually, my first real business enterprise of any kind outside the orchestra. The very next day, as I recall, I went down to see Mr. Volk and we talked over our mutual needs. A few weeks later he telephoned to say that Union Bank was definitely interested, and would like to occupy the first two floors of our proposed building. That made it possible for me to build a much nicer structure than the one I had dreamed about. Instead of two stories, we could build six—two for the bank, one for us, and three to rent out. I had started out to build a simple little office building to take care of our needs. And look what it had led to!

Ed and Ted, as I outlined in the preceding chapter, handled the actual project. Once I got the ball rolling, I turned it over to them completely. All my life, I've made it a practice to find people I can believe in—and then *believe* in them. And when I turn over a project to anyone, that's exactly what I do, give them full responsibility. For me, that philosophy has worked very well with many people.

The day we dedicated our first building provided a real thrill, and a bit of a surprise too. Our public relations expert, Les Kaufman, who's another member of the "family," having been with us for over a quarter of a century, came up with an idea that tickled everyone. Unbeknownst to me, Les rigged up a pipe just beneath the surface of the earth where I was scheduled to turn over the first spadeful of ground. Just as I did, he pressed a button, and a mountain of bubbles exploded into the air, drenching me, the building, and everyone present! It looked as if I had shoveled up a bubble machine for sure.

Ted and Ed did such a superb job handling this first project that we were able to acquire another choice piece of property a few years later. It was a prime number one location in my opinion, a corner lot at the junction of Wilshire Boulevard and Ocean Avenue, commanding an unparalleled view of the Pacific Ocean, with the grassy esplanade of Santa Monica Parkway just across the street, its tall palm trees waving in the sea breezes.

When we first bought it, there was a gas station on the corner and a thirty-two room apartment-hotel next door. We retained it just as it was for the next few years. The orchestra was continuing to do so well, we weren't pressed to do anything about the property, and the rentals paid for the taxes and maintenance. Over the years, we had a number of suggestions to build a hotel, motel, nightclub or restaurant. But none of them seemed quite right for this exceedingly beautiful spot.

One day, however, George Thomas came back into my life, and—luckily for us—introduced me to Parker Sullivan, who was then president of the General Telephone Company. Mr. Sullivan came to see me and told me his company was looking for a place to establish their expanding company headquarters. He thought our property might make an ideal location for them.

We began looking into it, and it developed that the General Telephone Company would need about fifteen floors of a proposed building. That meant we would be able to construct a truly impressive twenty-one story office building, plus an adjoining sixteen-story apartment house.

At that point, I again turned the whole huge enterprise over to Ted. He and Parker (who became a dear friend as well as a prized golf competitor) worked together for several years to bring their sketches and dreams and plans into reality. The General Telephone building and our Champagne Towers apartment building—the first two units of our Lawrence Welk Plaza—were dedicated in 1971. Ted and Parker, in partnership with the architectural firm of Daniel, Mann, Johnson and Mendenhall, had done a truly magnificent job.

But that wasn't all. In 1979 Ted walked into my office with the result of several more years' labor on his part—getting together plans and permission to construct the third part of our complex, an office building on the other side of the Champagne Towers, a breathtakingly beautiful edifice (or at least it seemed so to me) constructed in a receding "stair-step" fashion so no views were obstructed, and a great deal of greenery could be incorporated. (You can see a model of it in the picture insert.)

Ted had worked very hard on the entire project and, particularly so I think, on the third phase of it. And when he stood on the other side of my desk, pointing out all the details on the mock-up of the completed complex, I felt a tremendous surge of pride in his accomplishment, and great joy, great gratitude.

I had always wanted Santa Monica to be "proud" of me. They had taken me in, so to speak, when the boys and I first opened at the Aragon, and through the years we had grown together. It has been my home for years now, and Ted and I have always enjoyed a wonderful relationship with the other businesspeople in the community, and with the city fathers too, who made it possible for us to create these beautiful buildings.

I had wanted to leave something permanent, a monument, something of value to the city and the nation which has been so good to me. Now, looking at these tall white towers, put together with such loving attention to detail, I felt perhaps we had.

12.

Our Office "Family"

Our business interests have expanded steadily over the years, but even so I've always considered myself in the small-business category. We may be slightly over the mark, however. We've gone from an orchestra of seventeen members in 1951, to one of over fifty in 1979; a staff of seventeen in our business office in Santa Monica; another one hundred and sixty in our Escondido operation; and a backup staff in our various other projects, which brings our total number of employees close to three hundred.

Our business office in Santa Monica is the nerve center for all our operations, and whenever I'm in town I'm there every morning till "golf time." The office is located on the seventh floor of the General Telephone Company building, and I get there every morning about 7:15—one of the first to arrive, as you might suspect. I ride up in the elevator to the dark and silent seventh floor and let myself in to greet whoever is there. Usually Dean Kay, head of our publishing division, and Virginia

Burnham, our dedicated controller, are the only ones around. At 7:30 I telephone Bernice to check over the day's writing plans, and then meet with the rest of our business "family," who begin coming in very quickly. By 7:45 they're generally all present and accounted for, and I'm having coffee (again, it's tea for me) in the little kitchen-lounge at the rear of our suite with "the girls," my name for the four young ladies who divide up the secretarial duties in our office: Laurie Rector, Barbara Curtiss, Margaret Heron, and Julie Jobe. But let me tell you about them separately, because to me, they're all "daughters," all part of our big extended "family."

Laurie became my secretary when her sister Lois Lamont, who had been with me since 1945, suffered two severe illnesses and had to curtail her time at work. Laurie took over the job of scheduling my appointments, handling phone calls, and making sure I remember to take whatever it is I need when I leave the office for the studio, or anywhere else. She has such an infectious laugh we all enjoy it, and she has done a superb job of handling an unexpected and intricate job. As a secretary, she's just what the doctor ordered. I used to think no one could equal Lois, but Laurie is so good I'm beginning to think that dedication and superior work just run in the family! Lois, by the way, is now general executive secretary for the entire corporation.

Then there's slim little Barbara Curtiss, who helps me so much with my letters. She's so brilliant she almost embarrasses me. Barbara keeps track of our fan mail—what the audience likes and doesn't like. In fact, she keeps what she calls a "fever chart," which lists the names of all the performers, what kinds of compliments and catcalls they get, what kind of music is most popular (and isn't)—that kind of thing. Our fans are almost an information service for us. They report when certain stations "bump" us off the air, and mail us copies of the letters they send in protest. One of the main reasons for our success has been the devotion and support of our fans, and they are a tremendously important part of our daily business life. What they think and what they want is of vital importance to us—and Barbara's "fever chart" makes it all instantly available and instructive.

Incidentally, this may not be the time to tell you, but Barb and the other girls often cull out some of the funnier song requests from the letters. Fans will write requesting their favorites, but they don't always get the titles right. We have a list of some of the funnier bloopers. Some of my all-time favorites are "Let's Make Hay While the Sun Shines, Nellie" (instead of "Wait Till the Sun Shines, Nellie"); "Dr. Chicago" (for "Dr. Zhivago"); and "Wedding of the Tainted Doll" (for "Wedding of the Painted Doll")!

Margaret Heron is our living memory bank. This lovely young lady, who came to us fresh out of high school, knows exactly where everything is without looking it up. What a mind! Just remarkable. She handles the actual production of our mail input and output, and does a flawless job. We couldn't do without her.

Julie Jobe, at our reception desk, has the same lilting and friendly voice that won her the job in the first place, and wins friends for us the moment she answers the phone with a cheerful, "Good morning, Teleklew, Julie speaking!" Julie is also famous (with us, anyway) for her ability to track down people we're trying to reach.

These are the four girls who answer when you

call us, or help me answer your letters, and they have developed an esprit de corps as good or better than that in the orchestra. They really *care* about the show, and whether we're doing the best possible job, and how we can please our audiences more. They care about the company and each other—and me—with a devotion that leaves me almost breathless with gratitude.

But I find that same spirit of cooperation and fierce determination to do the best job possible in all the departments of our organization. Right next to my office suite, for example, is Ted's, with two adjoining offices—one for his brother Jack and one for his pretty and efficient secretary, Brigitte Jennison.

I might tell you a little story about Brigitte. She had been with us only a short time when I heard she was a fine dancer. So one morning I buzzed her and asked if she'd come in and take a letter. "My own girls are all busy at the moment," I told her. "Certainly, Mr. Welk," she replied, and in a moment walked through the door with her pad and pencil in hand. But I didn't dictate a letter. Instead, I jumped up from my desk, walked across the room to meet her, and before she knew what was happening, began waltzing her around the room to the strains of the Viennese Waltz I had just put on the stereo! Poor Brigitte turned bright red, and I'm sure she must have wondered what kind of crazy place she'd gotten into. She is a very fine dancer, by the way, and tells me her father taught her when she was a small girl. So there's another "argument" for early training.

I might just mention that as Ted's duties became more and more complex, he needed more help, and he suggested that perhaps his brother Jack might be willing to assist—(these Lennon brothers are certainly devoted). Jack was then sixty years old and had recently retired from an illustrious career as a Foreign Service Officer at embassy posts all over the world. There are a host of commendations from top leaders of this country on the walls of his office, and no wonder. Jack is a tall courtly gentleman of great charm, and he had done an expert job of management responsibility for all government operations in France and the Philippines, including consular missions and government construction and leasing. Both Ted and I felt he would be ideal to head up our real estate interests.

Jack was pleased to be asked, grateful that he had a chance to work and use his talents. He was beginning to be bored stiff by his retirement! It bears out my feeling that all of us, at *any* age, should be allowed to work if we want to, if we can find jobs we want. All those legal restrictions just cause unnecessary complications and stunt our personal development. I don't see any reason why we can't keep growing till the day we die, and I believe it's wrong, almost shameful, to stop ahead of time. And if Jack was pleased that we asked him to join us, I'm delighted that he accepted, because he has helped infuse our company with new visions, too.

Right down the hall from Jack is Dean Kay's office. He arrives about 6:30 every morning and goes right to work telephoning people back East, where it's already 9:30. Our Welk Music Group now has branch offices in Nashville, New York, and London, and Dean is doing a marvelous job of administration. You might be interested to know that he also wrote "That's Life," the big Frank Sinatra hit. So he's talented as well as brilliant. Willa Hubert, George Thow's lovely daughter, is Dean's assistant, heading a group of five very dedicated young people.

Across town are two more people who are a big part of our business life—a very big part! In Hollywood is Sam Lutz, who's been my manager and agent forever—or at least it seems that way. "Sammyboy" has been with me since the forties and has done a truly wonderful job—always there, always helpful, always supportive. And out in the San Fernando Valley, in Studio City, is Don Fedderson, the man who launched us into national television in 1955 and syndication in 1971. He, too, has done a brilliant, a wonderful job for us.

Visitors to our office very often comment on the relaxed atmosphere. I have to agree with them. Partly it's due to the surroundings. There are magnificent views of the Pacific Ocean from almost every window, there's soft music playing in the background at all times—I guess I just couldn't live without music— and there are soft jokes and laughter coming from various corners, especially from "the girls," who have a wonderful rapport. But mainly, I think, the relaxed atmosphere comes from the fact that we're all working toward the same goal, and the consequent lack of tension among and between us helps us get things done easily and smoothly.

Our orchestra, our business office, and our publishing interests are three of our most important enterprises. But there's one more which is very, very close to my heart—Escondido.

POSTSCRIPT: "Barbara's Fever Chart." I thought you might get a kick out of seeing a few more of the slightly garbled song requests we've received in the mail, so here's a partial list for you.

Cow Cutter	(Calcutta)
Aisle of Capri	(Isle of Capri)
Bronze Lullaby	(Brahm's Lullaby)
White Clips of Dover	(White Cliffs of Dover)
Bessa Ma Moocho	(Besame Mucho)
Springtime in the Rookies	(Springtime in the Rockies)
Dunker Shane	(Danke Schoen)
V O Can Go My Darling	(Vaya Con Dios)
Twenty-nine Trombones Fourteen Trombones	> (Seventy-Six Trombones)
Wheel Barrel Polka Bear Bell Poke	> (Beer Barrel Polka)
Tip Top Through the Tulips	(Tip Toe Through the Tulips)
Sam Lewis Blues	(St. Louis Blues)
Jack the Knife	(Mack the Knife)
Bubbles in the Wind	(Bubbles in the Wine)
Chitty Chitty Whiz Bang	(Chitty Chitty Bang Bang)
When You Walk Through a Store	(When You Walk Through a Storm)

and more and more!

13.

"People"

_____ _ℐ_

On August 5, 1978, Fern and I sat at the head table at a
wedding reception in Escondido. It was beautiful. There was a
long buffet table against one wall, decorated with silver
candelabra and white roses, and laden with ham and turkey
and roast beef. There was an elegantly impressive four-tier
wedding cake. There were waiters passing trays of champagne
and tea and coffee. At one end of the huge banquet hall, a dance
band was playing everything from salza to disco to polkas.
Overhead, bubble chandeliers lighted the room, while behind
us, floor-to-ceiling windows overlooked the velvety green lawns
of the golf course and the rugged mountain terrain beyond.
Everywhere I looked I saw beauty and happiness. And at the
center of the table was the radiantly beautiful young lady
whose wedding this was—Mrs. Rudolfo Eccheverria, better
known to you and me as Anacani.

      She looked exceedingly beautiful that day in a
gown and headdress of white lace and seed pearls,
which she had designed herself. Beside her sat her

handsome groom—so proud of his lovely bride! As I
watched her greet her many friends with such poise and
grace, I could feel my eyes starting to fill with tears.
Anacani had been just a little girl when she had bumped
into me—quite literally—only five years before. I had
been coming out the door of our Village Inn Restaurant
just as she was walking in, and I had been so impressed
with her vivacity and outgoing personality, as well as
her beauty and talent, I hired her immediately, as our
first Singing Hostess. For the next few months she had
commuted from Escondido to Los Angeles, working
both in the restaurant and on the show, and she had
done a superb job on both, becoming one of our most
loved and popular stars. Now she was back again in the
restaurant where it all began, sharing her happiness
with the friends she had made along the way. I was
indeed very, very proud of this truly lovely young lady.

      I've always believed that "people" make the
difference in any venture, whether it's an orchestra, a
television show, a publishing company, or a restaurant-
motel. Anacani had certainly been one of the people
who helped us most at Escondido, but there were others
there that day who had helped enormously, too—genial
Paul Ryan, the wonderful man who managed our
restaurant; Bill Balnaves, our matchless chef, and his
lovely wife, Arlene, who works so closely with him;
Adriene Edwards, the sparkling young lady who has
been with us from the beginning. Adriene has such a
wonderful sense of humor she's a show all by herself.
No matter what you say to her, she has an answer, and
it's usually pretty funny. You folks may have seen all
these people on one of our specials from Escondido. All
of them were there for Anacani's wedding, along with
friends from the motel office, the golf course, the gift

shop and, of course, friends from the show. It seemed to me I was surrounded by some of the people I knew and loved best in the world that day.

Bert Carter of course—(Bert is the man responsible for getting me on television in the first place. He was with Dodge when his wife, Nancy, "found" us at the Aragon Ballroom in Santa Monica. Next thing I knew, we were on TV!) Bert also helped me find Escondido. As I mentioned in my book, *My America, Your America*, he and Ted Lennon and I were driving by the place one day when I spotted a pretty little golf course running through the grounds. I insisted on turning back and am I glad I did. Escondido has turned out to be one of the highlights of my life.

It was relatively small when we found it— there were about twenty-five mobile-home spaces, a four-unit motel, a clubhouse, a tiny restaurant, and a three-par, nine-hole golf course. I really had no plans to expand it. I just fell in love with the climate (considered to be one of the best in the world), the beautiful countryside—and that golf course! Bert agreed to manage the park for us and for the next few years, he and I and Ted were constantly dreaming up new ideas on how best to develop it for our friends and fans.

We almost had to, because right from the start our fans began visiting us in such great numbers, the little four-unit motel couldn't begin to take care of them. I remember counting license plates in the parking lot one afternoon, and there were cars from twenty-three different states. So, first we enlarged the motel. Then we added a swimming pool and a Jacuzzi, enlarged the restaurant, added nine more holes to the golf course, built a gift shop, and added another motel—and one day it dawned on me, we had ourselves quite a place.

By 1978 the rush of visitors had become so great we went ahead with another major expansion, adding two hundred fifty more mobile-home spaces, another clubhouse, another swimming pool, tennis courts, another motel—and there are even plans to add a Welk museum and theater! My head swims just thinking about it, and sometimes the size of the expansion scares me. But it also pleases me to think that perhaps some of the memorabilia and mementos from our past—some of the history of the band itself—will be on display for years to come for our fans and friends to enjoy.

We had a few troubles in the beginning, I must admit. I had one restaurant manager in the early days who kept telling me I should hire a mariachi band to liven up the place.

"I don't want to liven it up," I told him. "I want it to be a nice, quiet, relaxing dining room, serving the best possible food."

"Oh, but the people would love it," he persisted. "It would add a lot of excitement."

"No," I said positively, *"no music"* (unless, of course, it was Lawrence Welk music playing very softly in the background)!

I guess he didn't hear me. A few days later he called and said, "You've gotta come down here, Mr. Welk, I've got a big surprise for you!"

"Oh?" I said. "What's that?"

"I've just hired the greatest little mariachi band you've ever heard!" he announced triumphantly. "They're just sensational, you'll love them!"

"Now listen!" I said firmly, "if I come down there and find a mariachi band, you'll both be gone!"

The band wasn't there—and neither was that manager for very much longer.

In those early years I ran a survey and discovered that many of the residents in the area were on fixed incomes, so I decided to include at least one entree on the menu which they could easily afford. "I want a specialty that won't cost any more than if they fixed it at home themselves," I said. Some of my co-workers were doubtful. "Prices are so high, Lawrence," they said. "What could we possibly serve at that low a cost?"

Well, you know how I like to rise to a challenge. I thought for a while and remembered the good food we'd had on the farm when I was growing up. "How about chicken and dumplings?" I asked. "There are a lot of chicken farms around here—and how much could it cost to make a dumpling?" We found a firm in San Diego which could supply all the broiler-fryers we needed. Chef Bill experimented a little, and we finally came up with a chicken and dumpling dish for about $1.75. (Remember, folks, this was in the early sixties. Today the same dish is more than double in price. Inflation!) Our chicken and dumplings really caught on and are still one of our patrons' favorites. My favorite, however, is the custard Chef Bill fixes especially for me, on account of my sensitive tummy. I can eat only about ten percent of what most folks eat, so Bill always takes pains to have a pan of custard ready when I arrive. Nobody makes it better than he. Except for Fern, of course.

I go to Escondido as often as my heavy schedule permits, for some relaxation, some golf, a little fun, some visits with our long-time tenants. Very often when I leave my home in Santa Monica early in the

morning it will be dark and foggy (the Los Angeles
Chamber of Commerce won't like this, but it does get
foggy here once in a while). I'll start driving down the
Coast Highway toward Oceanside, about eighty miles
to the south, and it will be damp and foggy all the way.
But at Oceanside I turn inland on Highway 76 to
Gopher Canyon Road, and, about six miles away from
our Country Club Village, I drive right out of the fog
and into brilliant sunshine! No wonder I love it. And
the countryside is so very, very lovely—rolling hills
planted solidly, mile after mile, with acres of avocado
trees, orange or lemon groves, beautiful flower farms,
strawberry fields, mushroom farms, chicken farms.
And there are several small guest ranches nestled into
the foothills behind white split-rail fences, with horses
grazing contentedly in the background. It's not only
delightful, it's very homelike as far as I'm concerned—
the place is surrounded by farmers!

Not long ago I drove down for a weekend visit
and walked into our restaurant very early in the morning for my usual waffle only to find the place already
crowded. All the seats along the big picture windows
were taken, the sunshine sparkling on the lake, the grass
shimmering from the early morning dew, tiny hum-
mingbirds flitting by the windows and perching on the
feeders hanging outside the windows. It was such a
beautiful sight and such a beautiful morning, I went out
to my car, got out my accordion, and surprised everyone
by going around from table to table playing, "Oh, What
a Beautiful Morning!" I love to play for the folks, I
really do. I tell Myron that ever since I hired him, I have
to play wherever I get the chance, because they won't
let me play on the show anymore. Well, that may not be
exactly the case. But it is true that I like to play directly
for the people. It helps me keep tuned in on what they

really want and keeps our lines of communication open. So as long as they'll listen—I'll play!

I feel very good about the success of Escondido, because from the very beginning we tried to establish "quality" as the hallmark of the place—that was my big argument with the manager who wanted the mariachi music. I wasn't against the music—well, hardly, considering my background—but I was determined to build a reputation on food rather than entertainment. Bill Balnaves and Paul Ryan were with me one hundred percent in this respect, and Bill spent hours perfecting new recipes and personally training his help—two of his assistant chefs today, started out as his dishwashers. Bill is most certainly a practitioner of our "family" concept. So in spite of the fact that Escondido has almost quadrupled in size since we took over, we have been able to retain a nice, warm, family feeling.

That seemed so very apparent to me on the day of Anacani's wedding. Earlier, we had all met at St. Mary's Church in the city of Escondido for the wedding Mass itself, a very moving ceremony conducted by young Father José, partly in Spanish and partly in English. The church was filled to capacity with friends of both families, as well as friends from the band and the restaurant. Later we formed a caravan and drove back to the restaurant for the reception, and I sat there watching that happy, laughing throng, hugging and kissing each other, having such fun together, it struck me that this was no gathering of employees who had dutifully assembled to witness the wedding of a coworker. This was a gathering of the clan, who had gathered together in love to celebrate the wedding of a favorite daughter.

And in truth, that's what it was.

Part Four

Our Way of Life

14.

Sharing

When I first started writing this chapter, I thought I had an absolutely brilliant way to dramatize how successful our profit-sharing program has become. I was planning to tell you exactly how much each of our people receives as his share of the profits. But after thinking it over, I realized I just couldn't do it. It wouldn't be right, it would be an invasion of privacy, and of course that is something I could never ever do.

Actually, profit sharing is only one small part of our total sharing program anyway, because we share a great many other things besides profits. But profit sharing is certainly an extremely important feature, and one which, I think, becomes increasingly important to our people as they grow older. I don't really think our new young people give it much thought at first. They understand they'll share in the profits after they've been with us for one year. But it isn't till they've been with us a while and had a chance to learn how much some of the older members have been able to accumulate through profit sharing, that they tend to become very, very interested indeed!

As I said, I cannot in good conscience reveal what each of our people receives. But I think I can give you a generalized account of our entire profit-sharing program which will give you a pretty good idea.

For example, as I write these words, we now have a little over five million dollars in our Employees' Profit-Sharing Fund. All this money is contributed by management. We have taken amounts equal to fifteen percent of our total annual eligible payroll, and deposited them in a special fund which is maintained and invested for the sole benefit of the employees. It is their fund, and each employee receives a percentage of his total annual salary as his share of the profits.

This is a great way to motivate people, I must say. Somehow, when you know that the better you do your job, and the more valuable you make yourself to the organization, the higher your share of the profits— you just naturally begin doing a better job!

As to the exact share our people receive, again I must tell you I cannot invade their privacy. But I think I can safely say that if certain people were to leave the band today, they would take with them amounts varying from ten thousand dollars to three hundred thousand dollars—or more—as their share of the profits, depending on how long they've been with us and what their status in the organization has been.

I must confess it gives me a very, very nice feeling to know we can provide our folks with this kind of security. Some of our long-time members, for example, have well over one hundred thousand dollars to their credit in this fund, in spite of the fact that none of them are what I'd call solo performers. That makes me very happy. It used to bother me terribly years ago when I'd see some of the boys save up for a few years and then lose all their money in some "get rich quick" scheme—musicians are not notorious for their business ability! I worried about it, trying to figure out a way to provide some solid security for them at the time in life when they would really need it. I believe our profit-sharing program is the answer, because none of our people receives his share till he leaves or retires, and that's generally the time when a little extra cash comes in very handy.

It gives me a good feeling to know we can help in this way, but it's entirely consistent with my feelings that "the fruits of their labors should go to those who earn them." I've always believed that if people are willing to share the hard work of trying to reach a goal, they should share in the rewards too. To me, that's simple justice.

But, as I said, profit sharing is really only a small part of our overall concept. With us, sharing is a state of mind, an attitude, a philosophy of life, and we share constantly in many, many ways. For one thing, we share by giving gifts and bonuses throughout the year for unusual or outstanding services, or for simply maintaining a high level of performance, as so many of our members do. But so often they go far beyond the call of duty—Jack Imel, for example, always knocks himself out on tour, making sure every little detail is exactly right; little Mary Lou Metzger not only spends hours getting her own act together, but does things like drawing out the steps on a piece of paper for me to study before we do our dance number together. Barney Liddell is always there, always willing, always saying, "I'll get it, Boss!" or "I'll do it, Boss!" no matter what the situation is. It seems to me that our people go out of their way constantly to do a superior job, and it's a great, great pleasure for me to share our joy and gratitude with them through gifts or bonuses.

People often ask me what kind of gifts we give, and I never know what to say, because we've given everything from lawn furniture to a stereo set, from cash bonuses (very high on the popularity list, I must admit) to vacations at our homes in Palm Springs and Escondido, from car-leasing arrangements to a deferred cash payment. It could be any one of a hundred things, but always something suited to the person's real needs or desires. One of my most pleasant "duties" is to try and figure out just what will please a certain employee most. We've picked up mortgages, assigned a financial consultant to get somebody's budget back in working order, sent people on vacation trips, paid for wedding receptions. There's really a limitless range as to what we do in the way of sharing.

I tend to look at promotions within the company as a way of sharing too, and I love to throw new challenges at people (also an excellent way to teach them and help them expand their knowledge). I might ask them to try their hand at some arranging, for instance, or make a recording, or I might set up a personal appearance for them which will enhance their reputation and image—to say nothing of their bank account. Once you get into the spirit of the thing, it's amazing how many different ways you can come up with to share with your people.

Sharing goes far beyond the concept of dollars and cents. To me it means closeness, true friendship, a feeling that there is someone who cares, really and truly cares what happens to you and your life. I've mentioned in another book how concerned all of us were when Larry Hooper was so sick and off the show for four years; and again, when my secretary Lois Lamont suffered two major operations in less than two years. Just recently Curt Ramsey, our much loved arranger, underwent extremely serious eye surgery, and that was of great concern to all of us too. Larry, Lois, and Curt have each told us that the loving interest of everyone in the Musical Family was a great help to their recovery; and knowing there was nothing to worry about financially while they were off the show, helped significantly too. To us, sharing is caring. I honestly believe we think of each other as true friends, as brothers and sisters in God's family, rather than just as co-workers.

I would say to any employer that if you make a conscious effort to share your *life* as well as your business and profits with your employees, your life seems to become much, much brighter, and suddenly it becomes a pleasure just to get out of bed and get the day started!

All our sharing is based on the old biblical maxim: "Give, and it shall be given unto you."

And I might just interject here that when you "give"—when you— "share"—you're not really giving anything away at all. It all comes back to you in increased devotion, increased dedication, and a much finer, better, happier organization.

I see the truth of that demonstrated daily in the warm, close-knit feeling of love and commitment in our Musical Family. You can't buy that kind of feeling— you can only get it by giving it. As my dear friend Lon Varnell quoted one day, "Love isn't love till you give it away."

That's our concept of sharing exactly.

15.

Happiness

As you folks may possibly know, I've had to teach myself during my long life—and I'm still searching for knowledge. My library at home is jammed with books. I send for pamphlets that sound interesting, and I read every chance I get. I'm hungry for knowledge and to me, educating yourself is a lifelong process that provides tremendous stimulation and pleasure.

I talk to people from all walks of life in my quest for knowledge too. I've even asked my studio audience for advice. I come out about twenty-five minutes before show time every week to chat with them, and sometimes we get in rather serious discussions. One night, for example, I asked them what they thought was the most necessary ingredient for happiness. Hands flew up all over the studio! Everybody seemed to have the answer. But the answers turned out to be as varied as they were interesting. A great many folks said love was most necessary, and I agree; it is certainly important. Others said "a feeling of being needed" "respect" "religious faith" "peace of heart." (It was interesting to me to note that not one person mentioned money. I have a smart audience!)

Then the audience asked me what I thought was the most necessary quality, and my answer surprised them a little because I said, "Gratitude." But I feel very strongly that gratitude can bring great happiness in your life. When we're grateful, we are recognizing some particular good in our life, and that alone makes us happier. And when we show gratitude to others, it not only puts a nice, warm glow into their hearts, it puts an even warmer glow in ours. So I've always felt gratitude was a great aid to happiness.

And so is humility. Now I'm going to make a little confession about humility right here. When I first left the farm, I didn't speak English very well. The truth is, I could barely speak it at all! I didn't understand it very well, either, and for years I went around smiling brightly and pretending I understood everything that was being said. Every once in a while, of course, I'd get brave and say something, but more times than I care to remember, I used the wrong word at the wrong time and sent my listeners into fits of the giggles.

So I'd retreat behind my accordion and go home and study my prayer books some more. Eventually I learned enough to get by, but I still kept running into words that mystified me completely.

One time when the boys and I were just beginning to make a little name for ourselves, we played an engagement in Mitchell, South Dakota, at the famous old Corn Palace. Next day I went to Mass and then attended a breakfast given by the Knights of Columbus. After breakfast the parish priest made a little speech in which he mentioned our band and said that, in his opinion, part of our increasing success was because I appeared to be a humble man—one with true humility. I could tell by the tone of his voice that humility must be something nice; but I didn't have the least idea what it was.

I didn't want to reveal my ignorance, however, so I waited until I met the fellows and we began driving on to our next engagement. Then I said, casually, "Say, fellows, what does humility mean?" There were five other people in the car with me that morning, and I got five different answers. Not only that, they disagreed to the point where they got in a big fight about it. Some humility!

I decided to look it up for myself, but the dictionary left me even more confused, with definitions ranging from "a feeling of insignificance" to "the opposite of pride." It wasn't till several years later when I met the wonderful Bishop Fulton J. Sheen that I found what I thought was a very meaningful explanation. I was a big fan of Bishop Sheen—I've often thought we lost a lot when we lost him as one of our television friends. He and I talked at length, and he later sent me a collection of his books, and in one of them I found humility defined as "knowing the truth about your-self— and acting accordingly!" It was as if a bright light had turned on in my head. It seemed that I understood for the very first time just what humility really was. I think it's a fine definition. If you know the truth about yourself, the chances are pretty good that you're not going to be puffed up with pride!

No, humility helps you see yourself clearly, and brings a sense of balance and truth into your life. I would certainly include it as a quality that can bring happiness. But if I were asked to name the one essential for true happiness in this life, I would simply say: "God's Laws."

GOD'S LAWS

I personally love God's Laws—I'm completely sold on them. And why not? They've given me a life of such joy, such fulfillment, I am truly overcome with gratitude.

I was raised on those laws. We lived them—in my home, in our little community, and in our church and school. In fact, when I was quite young, I even boarded with the Ursuline Sisters at their convent in Strasburg. The daily trip to school from our farm into town was just too difficult in the wintertime, so all during the cold winter months, I boarded with the good nuns who had a great influence on me. My favorite was Sister Edith. How I loved her! She seemed to sense my feeling of inadequacy and my painful shyness, and she was so gentle, so kind and understanding. There were a few other children from neighboring farms who boarded in the convent, too, and I suppose we led a somewhat rigorous life—up very early for prayers, then a long day at school, then homework, more prayers, and an early bedtime. I remember particularly the pitcher of water that was left on my night stand for my morning ablutions. By morning the water was frozen, and I had to crack a film of ice to get to it. One time I confessed to Sister Edith that I really wasn't too keen about washing in that icy water every morning, but she just smiled and assured me it would make my cheeks rosy. She was right—it did! And my nose, too.

We children just absorbed the tenets of our faith from the good sisters and priest, and even as a very young child, I loved the strictness of it—loved the absolute quiet demanded in church, the obligation to fast before Communion, abstain from meat on Fridays, and attend Mass regularly on pain of mortal sin. Some of the rules scared me a little, it's true, but that was all right. They kept me on the straight and narrow, then and later—at least to the point where I didn't fall off entirely!

One time I did fall off a little, and I still get a twinge whenever I think about it. We had such a big family—eight children plus mother and father—that we sometimes took turns going to Mass, and one time, while my parents were at church, a couple of the neighbor boys and I got ourselves into mischief. Somehow we found ourselves down in the neighbor's cellar where there was a nice supply of homemade beer, and we decided to "borrow" some of it and drink a bottle apiece. The moment I got that last drop down, I began to suffer. Oh, how I suffered! I wasn't feeling any too good from the beer, but that was nothing compared to the sudden realization that I was going to have to confess this whole thing to our priest the following Saturday at confession. My stomach roiled at the prospect, because Father Max was notoriously strict under the best of circumstances. And now, with a real live shameful sin to confess to him, I knew I was in deep trouble!

All week I was in torment. I spent hours figuring out ways to tell my story so it would lighten up a little and not make me sound like such a black character. By the time Saturday and confession arrived, I was sick with nerves, but I marched off resolutely to the church where I stood in line waiting my turn, going over and over my story as I did so. But the minute I got into the darkened confessional, and realized the priest was waiting impassively on the other side of the partition, I just blurted out the whole story. Then I quaked on my knees, waiting for the ax to fall.

Wonder of wonders, it didn't. Instead, Father Max said very gently, almost as if he was sorry for me, "Don't worry, my child. It really wasn't as bad as you think. You're forgiven. Just promise never to do anything like that again." (Then he loaded me up with such a heavy penance, I was saying prayers for weeks.)

I was so relieved I nearly floated out of the church! I felt cleansed, reborn, forgiven, able to function again. And I realized dimly the power of confessing your sins, truly repenting them, and trying to do better. That, basically, is what I've tried to do all my life—meet and surmount temptation and try to do a little better each day. In the profession I chose, with liquor, late nights, plenty of money, any kind of pleasure you want easily available, it sometimes took a real test of will to resist all temptation.

But I was never seriously tempted, not to the point where I could abandon my principles and go against the teachings of my youth. The laws and ethics of God had been ingrained into me too deeply for me ever to go against them—and oh, how grateful I am today. How truly grateful. When people say that trying to live up to religious rules is too hard, I say, "No, that's not hard. It's trying to live *without* God's Laws that's hard."

I think people want them, really long for them. I hear folks calling in to talk shows looking desperately for some kind of guidance, some kind of help. Sometimes, when I listen to the advice they get, I don't know whether to laugh or cry. If only they would turn to God's Laws, they would find exactly what they're looking for.

But today our society has changed so drastically, people are often not even aware they're sinning. I'm deeply saddened at the complete breakdown of moral principles in our current life style, particularly our sexual morality. The total absence of any kind of restraints certainly hasn't made us happier. It has just complicated our already complicated lives. Our parish priest said recently that in the history of man there has never been a healthy, successful society that didn't impose definite sexual restraints on all its people. Conversely, every society which allowed complete sexual license has collapsed completely.

It makes me fear for the future of our country, our children, and our children's children.

In my opinion, we must hold on to the family as our strongest bulwark and our best protection. Just as I was writing this chapter, Fern and I went to one of our grandchildren's birthday party. It was the usual happy gathering of friends and relatives, but I couldn't help noticing how all our children clustered around Fern. Our three children and ten grandchildren adore her, as well they might, because she has devoted her life to them, being both mother and father when I was out on the road, and giving them the finest kind of example as a Christian wife and mother. On the way home, I told her how lucky we were to have such a nice family, and how lucky I am to have her. Fern's constant goodness, her stability and serenity, her wonderful ability to create a home for us no matter where we were have given us the roots, the security we need—and the love that holds us together.

It concerns me when I think about the number of children today who don't have a good home—who don't have a mother. Oh, they may have a mother, all right, but in more and more cases she's at work, either through choice or necessity. And nothing and no one can take the place of a good mother in a child's life! A sympathetic employer, an understanding teacher, friends—any of these can help. But nothing can replace a mother.

Of course there are women today who are not having children at all, who are trading a home and children for what they call "independence" or "career" or the "rights" that will make them equal to men. Now I've always thought women were superior to men in many ways, and here they are wanting to step down to be "equal!" Well, they may enjoy their independence while they're on the young side. But what about when they get to be fifty, sixty, seventy, or more? Where are the children who will love them? Where is the husband who will give them the love and respect they deserve as the mother of the family? I'm afraid that a lonely, bitter old age is in store for many young people who are unwilling to commit themselves to a marriage, a home, a family.

Now I don't mean to sound off against Women's Lib! I hire just as many women as anyone else in the music business. But in our organization it's understood that "families come first." We believe that's the way God meant it to be, and that's the way we want it too.

I've said many times that we rely on God's directives in our band. There's very little talk about religion in our orchestra. In fact, there's *no* talk—just action! I'm Catholic, many of our folks are Protestant, many are Jewish, and some may be other religions for all I know. We don't discuss it, we simply acknowledge the same basic, God-given precepts shared by every major religion, and probably exemplified best by the Ten Commandments. It doesn't take a genius to figure out what God's Laws are. And it doesn't take a saint to live up to them, either. It just takes someone with enough awareness to realize the eternal truth and power of those Laws—and the good sense to take advantage of them.

You can't get where you're going if you don't know where you're headed. God's Laws not only give you the goal, they point out the path, and give you a fully marked road map to follow.

POSTSCRIPT: I know that many of you folks are acquainted with the peace prayer of St. Francis of Assisi, but I thought I'd reprint it here for those of you who don't. It expresses so beautifully what I feel in my heart.

PRAYER OF ST. FRANCIS

Lord, make me an instrument of Thy Peace.
Where there is hatred, let me sow love.
Where there is injury, pardon.
Where there is doubt, faith.
Where there is despair, hope.
Where there is darkness, light, and
Where there is sadness, joy.

O Divine Master, grant that I may not so
much seek to be consoled, as to console;
to be understood, as to understand;
to be loved, as to love;
for it is in giving that we receive,
it is in pardoning that we are pardoned,
and it is in dying that we are born to eternal life.

16.

Welk Freedom System

So far in this book, I've talked about the importance of work and self-discipline; of freedom and sharing; the necessity of moral soundness; and the power of a strong "family feeling" in an organization. I don't know if it's been apparent to you, but those are the six basic points on which we have built our system—the one which has helped us achieve such phenomenal, long lasting, and personally fulfilling success.

Now I guess it's time to put the pieces together and explain exactly what our system is and how it operates—and why I am hoping so fervently that the businesspeople of our nation will become interested in it and give it a chance. Because if they do, they will be giving hundreds of thousands of deserving young people in this nation a chance too.

But before I do, I'm going to digress for just a moment and tell you how our system came into being. (I've told this story in my autobiography, *Wunnerful, Wunnerful!* and I'll recount it only briefly here. But it is important to an overall understanding of what makes our system tick.)

When I was young, I was a walking collection of weaknesses—so shy it was painful for me to look anyone in the eye or shake hands. As a small boy—and until my midteens, actually—I was always ailing with something or other, and when I was eleven, spent a full year convalescing from a peritonitis attack, following an appendectomy. I was the sixth child in a family of eight, and somewhat lost in the shuffle. Moreover I was quiet, a dreamer, thinking only of music, music, music! And if anyone had been asked to guess which one of the Welk boys would make it, I'm sure I'd have been last on the list.

When I left the farm at twenty-one, however, I had gained a little self-confidence because I had spent several years playing for barn dances and wedding parties in the neighborhood. But I still couldn't speak English, I had only a fourth-grade education, I was almost unbelievably naive and innocent, and I had a grand total of three dollars in my pocket. Not exactly the best set of qualifications with which to tackle the world.

On the plus side, however, I had boundless hope and enthusiasm. I'd been taught how to work on the farm, and I was a good, dependable worker. I could play the accordion. And above all, I ached to succeed! I was tired of being a nothing; I wanted to be a something.

However, I don't believe I would have made it except for two things: one, an unshakable belief in God's Laws, which kept me pretty much on the right track, and two, a man named George T. Kelly, who changed my life completely and set the scene for the system we use today.

Let me tell you just a little of what he did for me. To begin with, he hired me—much to my great joy, not to say astonishment—and then set about instilling in me every bit of self-esteem and confidence he could. He billed me as America's Foremost Accordionist. Of course I wasn't, but it made me play as if I were! He continually told me what a great star I could be, and how much he believed in me. He taught me timing, pacing, how to please an audience—everything he knew about show business, more than I could ever have learned in the finest dramatic school in the world. He continually raised the standards of what he wanted me to achieve, and encouraged me so that time after time I surprised myself and reached the goals he set for me. On only one occasion did George give up. That was when he tried to make an actor out of me. Even for George, a fine actor himself, that was an impossibility. I simply had no concept of what acting was all about— there weren't any actors in Strasburg. On top of that, I could barely speak English. But that didn't stop George. He wrote playlet after playlet which he thought I could handle. I'd try and fail, every time. So he'd write another one. I'd try again. This went on till he finally wrote a sketch ideally suited to my talents, a murder mystery in which a dead man was needed. All I had to do was lie perfectly still and not breathe when they lifted the sheet off me. Success at last. George said I was terrific.

That was the extent of my acting for the next forty years till Jack Benny tried to get me to do a dramatic sketch on his show. "Oh, Jack," I said, "I learned long ago that I'm no actor! I'm afraid I'd goof." "That's okay," said Jack, "that's my specialty. If you goof, I'll make a plus out of it." But the memory of my "acting" with George was still too fresh in my mind, so I begged off.

Then a few years later, Lucille Ball telephoned and asked me to guest star in her dramatic series; again I explained I was the world's worst actor. But Lucy wouldn't take no for an answer. "That's no problem," she cried, "you don't have to act. I've got the perfect part for you!" She talked it over with Sam and the next thing I knew I was on my way to rehearsal. Lucy was right. She *did* have the perfect part for me—a dummy! The whole sketch revolved around a dummy made to look like me, and all I had to say in the whole half hour was "wunnerful, wunnerful!" Lucy said I was terrific.

But to get back to George, he was a tremendous inspiration to me. He never allowed me to think of my limitations, only my possibilities. He spent hours with me, teaching me how to get along with people, and how to be at ease in social situations. He and his wife, Alma, patiently taught me enough English so I could study English prayer books on my own. He reminded me constantly that, in the eyes of God, I was as good as anyone else, and he shored up my self-confidence whenever it threatened to sag a little. In short, he helped me develop not only my talent—but myself as well. And on top of everything else, he shared his profits with me.

Now can you imagine just how that made me feel? I worked my heart out for him. I played the accordion better than I ever dreamed I could. I thought about our little show, "The Peerless Entertainers," all the time, and came up with new ideas which I hoped would help. George and I worked so closely together that I looked on him as a combination father, director, brother, coach, and dear friend. I believe he looked on me somewhat as his son. Together we accomplished the transformation of an awkward, shy, naive young farm boy, into a musician with enough confidence and know-how to successfully run a little band of his own. When I left George after two years of intensive apprenticeship, I had received the training of a lifetime. And the seed he planted in me has grown full-flower into the system we use in our Musical Family today. Over the years, of course, I added refinements and changes of my own to form our unique "freedom system," but I'm absolutely convinced that what George did for me—and what I'm trying to do for our people—could also be done by other businesspeople across the nation for the development of our younger generation. It would be a tremendous benefit to both.

When I'm asked to describe our system in one sentence, I have a little trouble. But if you can think of it in terms of a father or mother doing whatever is best for their children, you have a pretty good understanding of what makes it work.

I think of it also as an exciting new philosophy of business, although actually it's not new, but employs the traditional values of our founding fathers. Justice Mildred Lillie of Los Angeles, explained my feelings almost exactly in a speech she made to the graduating class of Pepperdine University, when she said that young people today should be guided by the fundamental disciplines that worked so well for our forefathers. She said, and I quote:

"In the early days of our international participation, our country was looked upon as a community of yokels—simple people who thrilled at the Fourth of July, bands and parks, fairs and circuses, parades and picnics and who actually cried with the joy and thrill of seeing our beautiful flag.

"Well, these yokels became the suppliers, feeders and bankers of the world. These yokels became the world's great technologists and scientists. These yokels brought not only security but comfort to, and uplifted the hopes of the downtrodden of the world. These yokels created great music, literature and art, and brought laughter and tears, through entertainment in all media.

"Why not return to the fundamental values and disciplines by which these yokels produced a valued society?"

I couldn't agree with her more. That is exactly how I feel.

Our system is based on those fundamental values. It is rooted in freedom, and believes in the power and accountability of the individual.

It motivates top performance, rewards excellence, shares profits, and bases all its actions on God's Laws. We don't have to wonder whether we're doing the right thing. God's Laws are always there.

Our system concentrates on building the people in our organization. And it answers the three basic human needs all of us hunger for: love, recognition, and a goal.

And it has worked miracles for us. I know that sounds like an overstatement, but it's the truth. It has simply worked miracles, keeping us together—and success-ful—in one of the most hazardous, rootless businesses in the world.

However, it could work much better if it were freed from the restrictions of the government and the unions.

That may sound like an impossible dream in this day and age—but why not? If people want to work together on a voluntary profit-sharing basis, and set up their own terms of employment—why not let them?

It wouldn't curtail the government or the union-dominated business organizations we have today. It would simply add to them—add a challenge, a choice, a new way to do business.

It would give our younger generation a more equitable chance to develop their talents—they could choose whether to work for the government, a union business, or a voluntary freedom system such as ours.

And something else occurs to me. Our govern-ment was created with a built-in system of checks and balances, to insure that no one person, or group of persons, would get too much power. Why couldn't the same idea be used in the business world? Voluntary freedom systems such as this could help us provide such a checkmate. I think it would make for a far more healthy condition in our economy.

I hope you who are reading this book will give serious consideration to these thoughts, these ideas; consider also how they could affect our future. I hope further, that any of you businesspeople who might be intrigued by our system, will analyze it to see if it meets the needs of your particular organization. Then, if you agree with its goals and fundamental precepts, I hope you will give it a try. You might be giving a helping hand to a young person who could later help the whole world with his talents.

Moreover, I'm reasonably sure that if enough of us businesspeople across the nation began using our Freedom System*—even under the present restrictions—it would go a long way toward helping us hang on to the freedoms we still have.

And maybe even save the free enterprise system itself.

---

*At the back of the book you will find a fully-detailed operating outline of the Welk Freedom System.

This may give you some idea of how long our people stay with us: Here are Curt Ramsey, Larry Hooper, and Dick Dale, as they looked when we were broadcasting from the Aragon Ballroom over KTLA in 1951.

Tom Mareschal

And here they are, thirty years later, with Sandi and Gail. That's Dick Dale at left; Charlie Parlato, our trumpet player, in the middle; Curt Ramsey at right; and Larry at the piano. They still look pretty good, don't you think? Champagne music seems to agree with them.

Our first real estate "venture," the Lawrence Welk–Union Bank Building at 24th and Wilshire in Santa Monica, across the street from the little park I was telling you about. Our office suite was on the top floor.

With Les Kaufman, our wonderful director of publicity for the past quarter century. He's the man who dreamed up the idea of me digging up bubbles, at the dedication of our first building. Les has done a superb job for us.

Toasting the beginning of the first two buildings in the Lawrence Welk Plaza: the General Telephone building and our Champagne Towers apartments. Left to right are Parker Sullivan, former president of the telephone company and now the retired chirman of the board, and also my golfing buddy; me; Ted Lennon; Bill Loors, the contractor; and Tef Kutay of the Dimjim Corporation, partners in the project. (I better confess that those glasses were empty. I never did learn to become a drinking man.)

Model of our addition to the Lawrence Welk Plaza.

The "girls"! Here is part of our office staff. Back row, left to right, Brigitte Jennison (Ted's secretary); Virginia Burnham, our faultless controller; and Margaret Heron of the fabulous, fantastic memory. Front row, Julie Jobe of the lilting telephone voice; me; Laurie Rector of the infectious laugh; and Barbara Curtiss, keeper of "Barb's Fever Chart." I forget what—or whom—we're laughing at, but it must have been funny.

At the groundbreaking for the Plaza, demonstrating I haven't gotten too far from the farm! That's Parker Sullivan next to me; if you look closely in the background you can see my secretary of 34 years, Lois Lamont, at left; then my writer, Bernice; and then Don Fedderson in the dark glasses.

My pleasant, relaxing vacation cottage, our mobile home-away-from-home in Escondido. The front door is just to the left of the lamppost, and there's a little fountain in the small garden at left. I love it.

Courtesy: Midnight-Globe

Chef Bill Balnaves in his fancy hat. That's our log-burning fireplace you see in the background, just off the lobby of our Village Inn Restaurant. Chef Bill and his lovely wife, Arlene, are doing a terrific job.

"Oh, What a Beautiful Morning!" Here I'm serenading one of the guests at our Village Inn Restaurant in Escondido.

Mr. & Mrs. Rudolfo Eccheverria, at their wedding reception in Escondido. (If I could read Spanish, I'd translate what it says on the heart. I wouldn't be surprised if it says something about love.)

Radiant Rose Weiss, who dresses all our girls so beautifully, chats with bride Anacani at her wedding reception in Escondido. "Rosie" does an absolutely phenomenal job of costuming our show. Not only that, she's a lady we all love.

You've heard of the Lennon Sisters? Well, here are the Lennon Brothers—and their lovely wives. Jack and Marjorie Lennon are at left, Ted and Peggy at right. Can you believe pretty Peggy is the mother of 13 children and grandmother of 23? We're in the patio-gardens of the Movieland Wax Museum in Buena Park, California.

Will the real Lawrence Welk please wave that baton? One of these figures is in the Movieland Wax Museum in Buena Park, California, the other in the Stars Hall of Fame, in Orlando, Florida. The other one lives in Pacific Palisades, California.

Courtesy: American Cancer Society

Some people who are closely associated with me: left to right are Myron Floren and Amanda Blake, co-chairmen of the Cancer Crusade for 1979; me; Mrs. Matty (Gila) Rosenhaus; Ardesh Zahed, the Iranian Ambassador; Lane Adams of the American Cancer Society; and Matty Rosenhaus, our incomparable sponsor. Matty has done so much to help the Cancer Crusade over the years and I feel greatly honored to have served as co-chairman on two different occasions.

Courtesy: American Cancer Society

Myron with beautiful Lena Horne, the Honorary Chairman of the American Cancer Society Crusade for 1979.

Some of those who joyfully celebrated my "Pepperdine" honorary degree with me: left to right, our eldest grandson, Robbie; his father, Bob; Bernice; our son, Larry Jr., with his sons, Kevin Phillip, 7, and Lawrence Welk the Third, 9; our youngest granddaughter, Lisa; our daughter Shirley; and Fern and me. This was a very happy day.

Justice Mildred L. Lillie, Mrs. Frank Roger Seaver, founder of Seaver College at Pepperdine, and Neva Hash, president of the Alumni Association, happy about the honorary degrees Justice Lillie and I have just received from Pepperdine University at Malibu, California.

Some of the people who
mean the most to me, are
the most camera-shy. I just
can't find pictures of them!
But here's one I found of
Lon Varnell, the wonderful
man who has taken us on
tour for the past 16 years—
I wouldn't go without him.
Here we are on tour
in Honolulu in 1971.

Here's the man who has made it possible for us to bring our
music to America; our wonderful sponsor, and my dear friend,
Matty Rosenhaus, with me on the Edgewood Golf Course
in Lake Tahoe, Nevada. All of us love and respect Matty.

And here's someone else who means a great deal to me—and she's even more camera-shy—my lovely wife of 48 years, Fern Welk. I have a terrible time getting her to pose with me, but I finally found a picture of the two of us getting ready to trip the light fantastic together.

My Musical Family. (That's our chief arranger, Bob Ballard, at my left, and musical director, George Cates, at the right.)

Tom Mareschal

Part Five

Our Country

17.

Some Recommendations

As you know, I feel very strongly about the child labor law, and in an earlier chapter I urged that we repeal it. I just feel that this law does serious harm to young folks who are trying to make something of themselves.

I happen to know a good deal about the child labor law because of my years of experience working with young talent—the Lennon Sisters, the Semonski Sisters, and other performers under the age of eighteen. I know what vexations and problems this law presents, and in our own case it has literally stopped us from hiring youngsters anymore. We have such a big orchestra that trying to get everyone rehearsed and costumed—get the whole show on and off the air in time—and still comply with all the demands of the child labor agencies, becomes a virtual impossibility. It's an unhappy situation for all of us, but it's the child who really suffers—he's the one who loses a chance to develop his talents and build his character.

I'm very aware of this because I constantly receive letters from youngsters who want to be on our show. I want so much to help them—but I just can't. There's a sensational fourteen-year-old country violinist, for example, who would be a delight to the nation, and I would love to have her on the show. I also have a tape and pictures of a sixteen-year-old soprano, a lovely young girl who not only sings beautifully, but plays piano well too. And I have a tape from three very pretty little girls from the South, who have an exceptionally fine vocal blend. These little girls range in age from 12 to 15, and are heartbreakingly eager to make something of themselves, but again I am virtually powerless to help any of these talented young people because all of them are under the age of 18. And we have learned, through long and trying experience, just how maddeningly difficult it is to try and fit the demands of social workers into our established rehearsal schedules.

The result is we've been practically forced to give up hiring anyone under the age of 18. The sad thing about youngsters like this being held back and kept from doing what they're really cut out for in life is that they sometimes lose their drive and enthusiasm. They just give up and settle for a mediocre life. Of course, there are always those youngsters who have such unusually strong character and determination that they'll make it, no matter what the setbacks. But the youngsters who aren't quite so aggressive—the ones who lose hope when the door is repeatedly slammed in their faces—they're the ones who need our help. Removing the antiquated child labor laws, which are not only costly but out of touch with the realities of today's life, would be an excellent way to open that door, and help our young people get started.

It's not only in my field that the child labor laws throw up such roadblocks. I would imagine that any employer in any field thinks twice before hiring a young person these days. The complications are just too severe.

There's another law which I believe harms our youngsters, too, and that's our minimum wage law. It has never seemed reasonable to me that a youngster should be paid a full minimum wage while he's still learning his trade—maybe even before he's learned how to work at all! No, it seems far more reasonable to adopt an open, more flexible wage scale during the training period.

I'm aware that there is now a graduated wage in effect for the training and apprenticeship programs instituted by the government in various parts of the country, but here again we get tied up in red tape. It seems to me that if any employer is willing to take a young person into his business, teach and develop him, and perhaps share profits with him, then the question of the training wage should be left up to the two people most closely involved—the employer and the trainee. I believe this would inspire many more employers to give our young people a helping hand.

In fact, I'd like to make a statement right now about our businesspeople. I feel they have not only been unfairly maligned, but are an overlooked source of tremendous good in our life. The businesspeople and the young folks in our country have a great deal to offer each other—an exchange of experience and energy that could enrich the lives of both. In fact, I might even go so far as to say the businesspeople of our nation could save our youngsters! The Good Lord knows that everybody else has tried—the schools, the government, various social agencies, churches. Everyone has had a hand in altering our social structures in the past several years, but somehow our youngsters are still getting involved in crime and drugs and teen-age pregnancies. My solution may sound simple, but I still say that if we gave our youngsters the opportunity to learn a trade through meaningful work, it would not only help them chart a path into their future, it would keep them out of trouble today.

Allowing our businesspeople—our competent, qualified, successful businesspeople—to help us guide and develop our youngsters at this crucial point in their lives might be the best thing we could do for them. For youngsters whose home life is poor, or nonexistent, a job with a sympathetic employer could even offer security, a haven, a home-away-from-home. It's certainly worth a try.

So I should like to recommend for our future betterment that we repeal the child labor law and consider revising the minimum wage requirements, too. Those two laws set up roadblocks in the path of youngsters who are trying to develop themselves—and I believe they should be removed.

But I must confess that the child labor and minimum wage regulations are only two in a long, long list of laws which don't seem to serve us well anymore. We appear to be increasingly hemmed in and surrounded by laws. There have been government surveys made which indicate the same thing—we simply have too many outmoded, irrelevant, and expensive laws on our books.

Well, I have something of a solution for that, too! My thought runs along this line: Why not establish a Blue Ribbon Committee of some sort to review all our laws, and recommend to Congress which ones should be retained and which ones discarded? What a breath of fresh air that would be! Membership on the committee would be purely honorary, a dollar-per-year type of thing. (That wouldn't break the budget!) Each member would serve for one year. The group would be composed of men and women of the very highest caliber, beyond any kind of political maneuvering, people whose only motive is the good of our country. Two or three representatives from each state would, I think, suffice to form a viable, workable committee. To me it's a practical solution which could help us break the stranglehold our outmoded laws now have on our freedom—and, our pocketbooks!

Basically, of course, I'd like to see us operating with a minimum of legal restrictions. I know we have to have laws to insure a smoothly running, civilized society. But I agree with Thoreau, who said, "That government is best, which governs least." I have long felt that the bigger and stronger the government, the smaller and weaker the people. On the other hand, when we are required—or allowed—to do things for ourselves, we become much stronger as a people, and, as a nation.

All my recommendations have one thing in common—a desire to build humanity. (I've been doing that for years in the orchestra. Now I'm ready to tackle the nation!) But that really is my motivation, that's what keeps me working so hard—to put into motion the acts that will eventually free our youngsters and allow them to work because, throughout my life, I have found work to be the passport to fulfillment and happiness. I realize there are several schools of philosophy in these matters, but I must confess that I am unequivocally devoted to the one that says, "You are free to develop yourself to the highest point of your potential—and you can *do it yourself!*" "Doing-it-yourself" teaches and develops you in ways that could not possibly be duplicated if someone else did it for you. And again, that's why I'm against any legislation that takes this privilege away from our youngsters.

18.

Do It Yourself!

I suppose I feel so strongly about the principle of "doing-it-yourself" because I've seen what it does for people. I would say, without question, that the best developed members of our orchestra all "do-it-themselves." And the boys and I certainly didn't learn how to operate the band or stay on television all these many years by relying on somebody else to do our homework for us! No, we were out touring the country for years, learning firsthand what the folks wanted, and how we could please them most. We blundered and floundered and fell down, that's true. But we got up again and kept on going, and I'm convinced we never would have made it without that hard experience. We not only learned what the folks wanted, we also learned patience, endurance, stability, determination, and how to make our product just a little bit better than somebody else's. That's free enterprise in action. That's America.

Even in personal ways, "doing-it-yourself" can have a powerful effect. Take my bad back, for example—and a few years ago I would have given it to you gladly!

My back problem started very suddenly one day, in the small town of York, Nebraska. The boys and I had played an engagement there, and next morning I began packing to get ready for a booking at the Hollywood Palladium in California. I bent over to pick up a small shoe bag—nothing heavy or unusual, just about the size of a shoe box—when suddenly I felt a twinge in my back. I paid little attention to it, finished my packing, got in the car and started driving. By the time we got to Grand Island, however, about forty miles away, my back was hurting so bad I could scarcely get out of the car. Then, after the boys helped me out, I couldn't get back in! I was mystified as to how this whole thing had happened. Surely a little shoe bag couldn't do all that.

We had three days to get to Hollywood and I can't recall a more miserable trip. My back was extremely painful and very stiff. Every so often the pain got so bad I would have to stop and see a doctor. Each one recommended something a little different. Some advised pills or shots or traction; a couple wanted to put me in the hospital immediately for surgery.

In Hollywood we opened at the Palladium, and my back got worse instead of better. It was really difficult for me to lean down from the stage to sign autographs or chat with our audience, and sometimes I could barely straighten up again. In desperation I went from doctor to doctor, seeking some kind of relief, but nothing helped till I found a doctor who prescribed neither pills nor surgery. Instead, he told me I had an ailment very common to businessmen who sit hunched over for long periods of time, perhaps at a desk, or driving long distances. He explained that a spinal column should be kept in a straight line, with each disc sitting lightly atop the other in order to distribute the weight evenly. He told me he thought my back could be cured to a large extent, but I would have to do it myself. "I can't do it for you," he said, "but perhaps you can." Then he handed me a little booklet called, "Ouch, My Back!" "Read this," he said. "It may help."

I read it and discovered it contained a series of exercises designed to strengthen my back. I did those exercises faithfully every single day for the next few weeks, and in a very short time, I began to notice a little improvement. After a few months had gone by, I realized—almost to my surprise—that my back trouble had gone, too! Today, my back continues to stay in pretty good condition, and I haven't had pain in years. (But I'm still exercising, just in case—you should see me touch my chin to my knees or roll up into a ball.) And I swim and play golf regularly, too. It all helps.

My point is that I had to do that for myself— no one else could do it for me. That's a lesson I'm so anxious for our young folks to learn. Actually, I believe they already know it instinctively. Most young people are itching to "do," to "act," to learn for themselves. The problem is we make it unreasonably difficult for them, with our child labor and minimum wage laws. And we stop them at just the time in life when they learn quickest and best.

It's too bad, actually, because we never really forget the skills we learn in our youth. I see that demonstrated constantly by the fine musicians in our band, nearly all of whom started playing when they were extremely young. I myself learned to play the organ when I was only about four, and today I play without even thinking about it. My fingers just skim over the keys in muscle patterns that have become a part of me. Same thing with dancing or playing the accordion or riding horseback or working!

But things I tried to learn when I was older—well, that's a whole different story! I didn't really begin swimming till I was in my fifties, for example, when Fern and I built our new home. We also built a pool, right off my bedroom, and the first thing I do every morning is jump, in for a few laps. The pool is twenty-seven feet long, and when I first started swimming, it took me eighteen strokes to get across. Today I can do it in four—well, make that four-and-a-half—I give myself a pretty good push. But I'll never be a really good swimmer, and you know why? Because I started too late, that's why. There were no pools in Strasburg when I was a kid.

Same thing with riding a bicycle. I bought a beautiful bike when we first acquired Escondido, and began riding around the lovely bike trails. That is, I tried to. But I had to give that up completely, too. And you know why? Because I got tired of all those skinned knees and bruised ankles. We couldn't afford bikes when I was a boy, either.

Our minds and muscles are most receptive when we're young, and I'm absolutely dedicated to the proposition that we should be given the privilege—or at least the choice—or learning at a very early age if that's what we want. The motor skills we learn when we're young stay with us all our lives. So do the social skills, which may be even more important—the art of getting along with others, of cooperating, of learning that reliability and honesty and truthfulness are not just words but qualities that must be employed if one is to live life successfully. All those things give a head start to the person who learns and uses them.

19.

The "Family" Comes Through

All the qualities we try to impart to our new young trainees come to the fore when we're on tour. If ever there's a need for patience, courtesy, good humor, tolerance, dedication, more patience, and just plain knowing what to do—it's when you're on tour!

Not that we don't love it. We do, and Lon Varnell, the Southern gentleman from Nashville who has arranged all of them for the past sixteen years, is a master at what he does. His arrangements are always as close to perfection as it's possible to be, but once in a while fate steps in and takes a hand. I don't think any of us will every forget the time in 1978 when we were in Pittsburgh, trying our best to get to Niagara Falls for the next show.

We were traveling by chartered plane on that particular tour, something we had been doing for about two years, and we were enjoying it too. It was very nice to have our own plane. It allowed us to sleep a little later in the morning and adjust the plane's schedule to ours, instead of the other way round. And on this particular tour, everything had gone as smooth as silk till we flew from Pittsburgh to Niagara Falls. That is, we tried to. We took off at one o'clock in the afternoon, but we hadn't been airborne for more than a few minutes when the pilot announced that a trouble light had flashed on his board, and he was returning immediately to Pittsburgh to check everything out. That was fine, that was only prudent; and after he landed, we all filed back into the airport and sat down to wait.

The pilot, who was also a mechanic, began fiddling around with all the dials and lights, trying to find out why that little red light had gone on; after about a half hour, I began to get a little nervous. One thing I hate to do is disappoint an audience. So far we haven't had to do it, and I didn't want to start that day, if I could help it.

I was considering just exactly what I *should* do, when suddenly it dawned on me I didn't have to do anything! My "children," our Musical Family—and Myron Floren, in particular—were doing it for me.

Myron had been watching the pilot check and recheck the plane, and on the possibility that it could not be repaired in time for us to get to Niagara Falls, he began inquiring around as to the availability of chartering another plane just in case. The only plane available at the Allegheny County Airport was a small six-seater. And we needed a plane big enough for forty-six.

Myron didn't give up. He kept investigating and finally contacted a charter company in Cleveland, Ohio. They had one plane available—a Convair seating exactly forty people. When Myron heard that, his hair stood on end just a little. He needed accommodations for forty-six people—and he had just found two planes which filled the bill exactly! He asked both plane companies to stand by for further developments.

I must confess I was having a terrible time just sitting there and saying nothing. It's in my nature to run things, to be the boss. But it's also in my nature to develop people and let them assume full responsibility. So I made up my mind not to say one word, and I did everything but bite my tongue and sit on my hands to keep from interfering. And of course I was tremendously impressed with the magnificent way Myron and the others were handling everything. Jack Imel, Barney Liddell, and Roger Sullivan (Ava Barber's husband) were all working like beavers. Myron had four pay telephones operating at the same time: one to Sam Lutz in Los Angeles, who was quietly going crazy trying to help out long-distance; one to the charter company in Cleveland; one to our travel service in Los Angeles; and one to the original plane company headquarters in New York. Myron was one busy Norwegian, running from one phone to the other as the fellows relayed messages to him. But he stayed cool, calm, and entirely unflappable. Just looking at his serene face made everyone else calm.

By 2:30 our wounded plane was still ailing, so we made our first firm decision. Lon and I would take off in the six-seater plane so there would be *somebody* on stage for the audience in Niagara Falls that night. As I recall, Jack Imel, who handles all our staging on tour, Bob Smale, Henry Cuesta, and Joe Feeney came along with us. When we left there were forty musical children still sitting around the waiting room of the airport—and not one of them complaining. They were reading or talking or laughing—some of them napping; but all of them handling this delay with great good humor and grace. I was very, very proud of them. But I was concerned, too. I hated to fly off and leave them sitting there, but there was very little we could do about it, so Lon and I and our advance group took off for Niagara Falls, flying through steadily darkening skies.

Meanwhile, back at the Allegheny Airport the weather had turned extremely bad. Thunderclouds were amassing, there were flashes of lightning, and fat raindrops (which presage a big storm) were beginning to fall. At three o'clock Myron reached the point of no return. Either he would have to have some assurance that our ailing plane could fly, or he would have to charter another one. When he conferred with the pilot and discovered he still had not been able to pinpoint the trouble, Myron decided to go ahead and charter the forty-seat Convair in Cleveland.

But when he telephoned to order it, he discovered the pilot of the plane had gone home for the day. "Oh, gosh," cried the girl in dismay, "the pilot just walked out the door to drive home! He's gone!"

"What!" yelled Myron. (I wasn't there, so I'm not sure he yelled, but I wouldn't have blamed him if he had.) "Well, run out and see if you can stop him!" "Okay," said the girl, "hang on for a minute!" Myron clutched the receiver while everyone clustered around him anxiously, and after what seemed like a very long time, a male voice came on the line and rather breathlessly identified himself as the pilot. "You caught me just as I was pulling out of the parking lot," he panted. He and Myron discussed the emergency, and the pilot advised it would take him fifteen to twenty minutes to check out the plane, and he would then fly immediately to Pittsburgh.

By now the weather was very bad. The big fat raindrops had turned into a pounding steady downpour, lightning flashed repeatedly, and when the Convair plane arrived about forty-five minutes later, it skidded through pouring rain to pull up beside our disabled plane.

Then everybody pitched in. Half the fellows in the band grabbed umbrellas and held them over the other half who helped Barney Liddell and Roger Sullivan assist the airport personnel in transferring luggage and musical instruments from one plane to the other. Back and forth they ran, sliding and slipping in the rain, dragging equipment off one plane and shoving it aboard the other. Then the fellows rushed back to the airport and with umbrellas held over groups of twos and threes, escorted all the girls out to the new plane. It was a quarter to seven when the big Convair finally took off. And show time was at eight o'clock!

In Niagara Falls I was all dressed and ready to go by six. Both Lon and I were very concerned at the thought of ten thousand people waiting in the Niagara Falls International Convention Center for a show to begin at eight o'clock, but I decided if worst came to worst, I could always take my accordion on stage and put on a one-man show for the folks, till my Musical Family arrived. I've had a lot of experience along that line. I thought I could get the audience clapping in rhythm, as my little friends at Macksville school had done, and I would dance with as many ladies as possible, or Henry Cuesta and Bob Smale and I could come up with some kind of number for the folks to keep them entertained. I was prepared!

Myron had kept us informed of his progress, and we knew he had chartered the second plane. We also knew approximately what time they planned to take off, and we were reasonably certain they would make it—the flight time involved was only about thirty-five minutes. What we didn't know was that the pilot would demand full payment for the flight before he would take off! Twenty-five hundred dollars.

Myron hadn't known that either, but it didn't stop him, even for a second. He just pulled out his checkbook and wrote a check for the full amount on his personal bank account. "Okay," said the pilot, looking first at the check, and then at Myron's transparently honest face, "we're off!"

The plane landed at the Niagara airport at 7:30. Lon had busses and taxis waiting to whisk everybody off to the hotel, where they rushed in, grabbed their room keys, stashed their luggage, and rushed right out again to the auditorium just around the corner. And at eight o'clock—as advertised—the Lawrence Welk Orchestra was sitting on stage, in full regalia, ready to go! Myron, looking as if he'd been relaxing in a sauna bath all day instead of racing around in a thunderstorm at an airport, played some of the most dazzling solos I've ever heard him play. All the kids came through with solid top-drawer performances. Not one of them complained or frowned or even yawned. They were much too intent on putting together the best possible show for our wonderful audience. Watching the girls—looking so pretty and fresh after their wearing experience—sparkle through their songs and dances, listening to the boys play with such a high degree of perfection, I felt again how lucky I was, and how beautifully our people were working together. We were certainly doing something right—and again I felt it was our system that was bringing out their great qualities of stability and maturity.

And I couldn't help reflecting on Myron's masterful performance getting that whole act together! He's had years of experience traveling, of course, not only with our show, but also on his own with thousands of personal appearances. During this past year also, he has toured the country constantly on behalf of the American Cancer Society, of which he is co-chairman along with Amanda Blake. He's in the air almost as much as he's on the ground, has come up against just about all the travel complications there are and learned how to handle them. When the chips were down that day he knew just what to do! Experience is the best of all teachers. And we had just seen a classic example of it.

POSTSCRIPT: In case you're wondering, we immediately repaid Myron for his "plane fare!" And there wasn't a thing wrong with the first plane. It was just a malfunction of the signal light itself! Water had gotten into the wiring system, and that's what had caused it to light up. Ah, well, it certainly made for an interesting day.

20.

Why I Wrote This Book

Sometimes I asked myself why I was so impelled to write this book. (I generally asked this when I got home from a hard day's work at 6:30, and Bernice was due to arrive at seven!) Certainly my friends and family were asking me, "Why do you want to load yourself up with so much extra work at this time in your life?" they asked. "Why don't you relax and take it easy?"

Well for one thing, I'm just not constituted that way. The key word of my life is ACTION, and if you took a look at my little appointment book, you'd see what I mean. It's covered with engagements for months in advance.

Fern occasionally tried to get me to take a little vacation, and once she even suggested taking a trip around the world. "Fern!" I cried, astounded. "Have you forgotten our trip to Europe?" She and I flew to Europe for a two-week vacation along about 1957, as I recall. Europe is beautiful, and we saw a lot of wonderful sights, but I couldn't wait to get home!

We had arrived in the middle of a heat wave, and this was in the years when air conditioners were not in plentiful supply. In fact, there were no air conditioners whatever in our hotel in Paris, so for the few days we were there, I went all over town looking for a fan or air cooler of some kind so Fern would be a little more comfortable—she has never been able to stand the heat. But oh my, what a time I had. I don't speak French (there are those who say I don't speak English either), and trying to make myself understood turned out to be impossible. I'd stagger back to our hotel utterly wilted from all the heat and frustration, only to find Fern relaxing comfortably in a nice, cool tub! My memories of Europe always seem clouded in a mist of steam heat, and I have no desire whatever to see the rest of the world. As far as I'm concerned, this country's got everything, and I'm perfectly happy to stay here and keep busy.

But it wasn't just because I like to keep busy that I wanted to work on this book.

Partly it was because I'm so concerned about the steadily dwindling supply of freedom in our country, the tremendous growth of big government, and the threatened loss of our free-enterprise system. These are things that concern us all, and I wanted to share my feelings and recommendations.

It seems to me, for example, that our government has simply grown past the point where it can function efficiently.

I'm not pointing the finger at anyone. I'm just stating the case as I see it today. We simply must take steps to reduce our government to a size where it can operate with more competence. And we must return to the people the right to participate more fully in the decisions which affect them on a daily, personal level.

But it's the plight of our young people that concerns me the most. Our youngsters are so fine, so full of promise. And yet somehow, they have become one of the most neglected segments of our society.

My recommendations for helping our younger generation are all based on the experiences of my own life. When I suggest that "work" may be a better choice for some youngsters than years of formal schooling, it's because that has been so effective in my own life.

When I say that removing the restrictions that keep our young people from working will open up their lives for them, it's because I've seen it happen time and again in our orchestra or other enterprises.

I don't want to *make* our youngsters work and I want to make that very, very clear. I just want to give them the opportunity.

I know that some people are honestly troubled by the thought that doing away with the child labor law would open the door for employers to harm our children. I don't think that will happen. For one thing, no youngster has to stay on a job one day longer than he wants to. If he doesn't like the job, or the employer, he can simply walk out the door.

And even if a youngster should run into an employer who treats him unfairly, or insensitively, he will still have learned something useful. (He will have learned how to be a better judge of human nature for one thing!) And he may have learned the basics of a trade or profession that can help him earn a living, or the subtle bits of information that can help him evaluate his future and make sensible choices.

So I would like to see parents encourage their children to work. I know our natural tendency is to shield our youngsters and protect them. But keeping a child from working—either in the home or out in the world—only postpones the day he discovers he must earn life on his own, only keeps him from developing the traits and characteristics he must have to live a successful life.

Basically, it was my affection and concern for the young ones that kept me busy writing another book off and on through the year. Very often I would sit in my library till late at night, poring over the books that mean so much to me, looking for a phrase or a thought to illumine my writings. And very often I would run across a key word or phrase that I had discovered originally when I was a young man, translating German into English. Those phrases had struck me with their truth and power then. Now as I read them half a century later, I realized how very true they were. "Give and it shall be given unto you." "Know thyself." "The Golden Rule." "Everybody's good for something; nobody's good for everything." "Blessed is he who has found his work."

All those phrases had a big impact on my life, especially the last one. I had found my work. I loved it.

Now I wanted to help other people find theirs.

So I kept right on working—and loving it. In February we wound up our television season for the year and then set out on our annual spring tour on March 1. And it was sensational, absolutely sensational, the best tour of our lifetime. Lon, as usual, had arranged the whole thing, and whenever he does anything, he does it right. Actually, he does it better than right, he does it perfectly! And this particular tour had turned out to be so successful than when Lon mailed us a check representing our share of the proceeds I was dumbfounded! I just couldn't believe it—I was so thrilled I even wanted to reprint it for you in this book! I thought back to the nickel-and-dime days when I had played not only for nickels but for just a bite to eat, and I realized what a long, long way we had come.

Lon has been responsible for so much of our growth. He's such a wonderful man. When people sometimes question whether a man can live a good moral life and still be a successful businessman, I wish I could introduce them to Lon. He's by all odds the most godly man I've ever known, and also, one of the most successful. When I asked him about it one day his answer didn't surprise me a bit, because I feel the same way myself. "Why, Mr. Welk," he said (we've been close friends for sixteen years, but he still calls me Mr. Welk, which gives you some idea of his humility), "Mr. Welk, the only way you *can* succeed in life is to follow God's Laws—and that goes for business or any other aspect of your life, as well." To which I have only one thing to say. Amen!

Over the years I have come to know Lon like a brother, and I am convinced that he would make an exceptionally fine leader for our nation. He has all the qualities we hope for in our leaders, all the qualities a truly great leader should have: integrity, a demonstrated ability to solve complex problems, independence from any kind of political ties, honesty, a brilliant mind, and rock-hard moral convictions. I've seen him operate successfully through one crisis after another, and always with total respect for and adherence to God's Laws.

Lon believes in self-government, as do I. He believes also that self-government comes only through self-discipline, and that the best way to solve our problems is to work on them ourselves, and not expect others to do it for us. He's a living example of the best in human nature, and the one man I know who could help our country get back the honest, effective, and moral leadership we are longing for.

People today have lost faith in our political

leaders, and most of us can certainly understand why. But there *are* honorable and able men in our nation. There *are* men and women of high principle willing to take on the crushing burden and responsibility of leading our country back to the moral stature we once enjoyed. We need only find them, and persuade them to run. I'd like to see us do that.

I'm indebted to Lon for thoughts which express his attitude as well as mine. Here is a list of some of the beliefs we share.

1. Work is the master key that opens the door to all opportunity. As long as the people of this great nation are willing to work, the American dream is very much alive.
2. Mental attitude plays a far more important role in a person's success or failure than does mental capacity. You have to have incentive. I don't believe anything can be accomplished without it.
3. The secret to happiness is not in doing what one likes but in liking what one does.
4. In evaluating a career, put a good opportunity above security. Have confidence in yourself. A person has to take risks to achieve.
5. People who take pains never to do more than they are paid for, never get paid any more than they do.
6. Don't procrastinate. In two days, tomorrow will be yesterday. Sell your wristwatch and buy an alarm clock.
7. Believe in God and obey his laws. There is a big exciting world out there. We can make it a little better by using our talents and sharing our blessings with others.

21.

A Week to Remember

After our March tour I settled down to the serious business of finishing this book. We'd had a little trouble, Bernice and I, in completing it, because I had been out of town so much in the preceding six months—either on tour, or on personal appearances or playing in a golf tournament. So when I got home from the tour I devoted nearly every night to the book, and we worked steadily for the next six weeks.

But there were a few very pleasant interruptions. In fact, during one particular week in April, it seemed as if there were just one wonderful honor after another!

It started on April 10, with a rather unusual affair in Buena Park, California, where I was officially "installed" in the Movieland Wax Museum in that city. Now I've had a lot of honors in my life, but that's the first time I've every been officially designated a "dummy." And after all the years I spent trying to live down my "dummer-esel" reputation from the farm!

Actually, no one every refers to those superb wax figures as "dummies" anymore and with good reason. They are actually masterpieces of the sculptor's art. Logan Fleming is the genius who makes them, and when I first saw mine, I couldn't believe it. It was so lifelike it was unbelievable. Even Fern, looking at a picture of me standing between two of my wax replicas, asked, "Lawrence, which one is you?" (There are two figures, by the way, one for the museum in California and one in the Star's Hall of Fame in Orlando, Florida, in case you'd like to stop by and visit us.)

At any rate, on the big day the officials at Movieland dispatched a limousine to pick up Fern and me and Ted and Peggy Lennon. When we arrived, they presented Fern with a beautiful white orchid corsage and me with a boutonniere, and Don Griffin, the handsome young mayor of Buena Park, presented me with a gold key to the city, too. Thank you, Mr. Mayor!

That was lovely, but what touched me most was to look out over the beaming throng gathered for the festivities and spot so many of my Musical Family who had driven down to help me celebrate my big day. I could see Barney Liddell, with a smile from ear to ear, and his lovely wife, Mary Ann; Johnny Zell with his beautiful young bride, Laura; Henry Cuesta's family (with little Henry, Jr., all eyes at the wax figures on display); Ken and Marilyn Delo, Bobby Burgess, Barbara Boylan, Rose Weiss, Curt Ramsey, and so many, many more.

Afterwards we all toured the museum, a big airy place filled with replicas of the great and near great. Our figure had been placed in a setting representing our television studio, and it stood, baton in hand, in front of a silhouette of the orchestra, looking for all the world as though I were leading the band. Later we relaxed in the patio garden of the museum for a leisurely luncheon, and it was such a pleasant day, so warm. The whole thing was fun—fun to be with my friends, fun to meet so many nice fans, fun to be "immortalized" in wax!

After that, it was back to work on the book again for the next few days till Saturday and another great honor. I was invested with an honorary Doctor of Laws degree from Pepperdine University in Malibu, California. I don't know when I've been more pleased. Pepperdine is not only an unusually beautiful school (it's situated on the hills above the Pacific Ocean at Malibu and is architecturally so magnificent it looks like a movie set), it is also an outstanding school both scholastically and morally, a church-related university which bases its entire curriculum on God's Laws. And of course that fits my philosophy exactly.

It was an exciting day in more ways than one. The ceremonies at the University were due to begin at 10:30 A.M., and by 8:45 Fern and I were all dressed and waiting for our son Larry to pick us up. But at five minutes to nine, the phone rang. It was Ted. "Boy, am I glad I caught you!" he said. "There's been a landslide on the Coast Highway between your home and Malibu, so you'll have to go through the San Fernando Valley and over the Malibu Canyon to get there." That would have been all right, except that Larry was at that very moment driving over from his home in the Valley! Two minutes later he wheeled into our driveway. I explained the situation to him and he turned right around and wheeled out again, heading back to the Valley, with Fern and me right behind him in our car so he wouldn't have to drive us back home. In the Valley we parked and transferred to Larry's car for the rest of the trip, with our two young grandsons Lawrence Welk the Third and Kevin Phillip (Kiki) chattering in excitement all the way.

"This is a fine thing," I said. "Here I am, just about to get the highest honorary doctorate of my life and it looks like I'll be late and miss the whole thing!"

Larry laughed. "I wouldn't worry," he said. "I think they'll wait for you."

Actually we arrived just in time, and it was a truly exhilarating sight as we drove up the broad curving highway to the Fieldhouse on the crest of one of the hills. There were banners and flags flying in the light breeze from the ocean; there was bright sunlight on the water; there were crowds of excited students, with black robes over their Sunday best; and a strong feeling of family love and hopes and excitement in the air.

Just before the ceremony I met with Dr. Howard White, the president of the University, and his staff of professors for a briefing. President White looked around the room at his group of erudite professors, all looking very impressive in their black velvet-trimmed robes, and explained just how to put on our mortar-boards. "You'll notice it says 'Front' in the front of the cap," he said with a twinkle. "And, gentlemen, that's where it goes—in the front!" We all chuckled, adjusted our mortarboards, and then began a long, slow pro-cession into the Fieldhouse which was jammed with family and friends of the graduates.

I must confess I felt pretty misty sitting on the stage and looking out over that assemblage. I was not only receiving one of the highest honorary degrees of my lifetime, I was also sharing the day with my dear family and friends. I could see our Shirley, looking so lovely, with her husband, Bob; their eldest boy, Robbie, handsome, tall, and strong at nineteen; their "baby," Lisa, now twelve. Larry sat with Larry, Jr., on one side of him, and Kevin on the other, and both little boys behaved so nicely all through the long ceremony. I was really proud of them—and surprised, too! Ted and Peggy Lennon were sitting with Bernice; my pals Eddie and Lu Shipstad were there; and, to my surprise and delight, so were my dear friends Meredith Willson and his lovely Rosemary, who turned out to be not only my friends but close friends of my co-honoree, Justice Mildred Lillie of Los Angeles. (Justice Lillie gave the baccalaureate address. It was so inspiring, I am quoting part of it in this book.)

After the investiture, we were invited to a lovely sit-down luncheon in the president's house, perhaps fifty of us in all. It was truly a wonderful occasion.

The next day—well, actually the same night— we went right back to work on the book again. But on Monday morning I took a little break for another high spot in my life. I picked up Shirley's youngest son, Jonathan, who is sixteen, and took him with me to Palm Springs for a rather special golf date. At least I thought it was very special. John Curci, of the Indian Wells Country Club in Palm Springs, had invited me to come down and play with President Gerald Ford at Arnold Palmer's Ironwood Springs Golf Course. I was delighted of course—honored to be invited—and the thought went through my mind that I had been privileged to play golf with two presidents of the United States, Dwight D. Eisenhower and Gerald Ford. Unbelievable.

Monday night I got all togged out in my best tuxedo and attended a dinner dance on behalf of the

Eisenhower Medical Center in Palm Springs. The dance was held at the Eldorado Country Club and was beautiful—good music, good food. Bob Hope and his wife, Dolores, were there; President and Mrs. Ford; my close pals, the Curcis and so many others. I had a beautiful evening—I always do if there's music and dancing—and I had a chance to dance with so many of the lovely ladies in our party.

But if that was wonderful, the next day was even better. Young Jon came along with me to be my caddy, very thrilled to meet the president. President Ford and I played against John Curci and Travis Whitney. (I'll keep our scores a secret. Let's just say John was a wonderful host and allowed Mr. Ford and me to share the winning score, and both the President and I were very pleased with it.) That was a real high spot for me!

But something happened the next night that topped the whole week. The phone rang about nine o'clock, and somehow, I knew instantly who it was. Sure enough, it was Don and Sam calling from New York, three thousand miles away, both of them so exuberantly happy I could almost see their grins over the phone. "Don," I said immediately, "what's happening?"

"Well, pappy," he said, "Sam and I have just finished talking with our sponsors—and it looks like you'll be working for another year!"

It's hard to convey how I felt at that moment. Thrilled, happy, jubilant, yes. In fact, the minute I finished talking with Sam and Don, I called George Cates and Jim Hobson and all my other right-hand people to tell them the good news. "And fellas," I said excitedly, "let's do the best shows of our lifetime next

year—the best! And let's start working on them right
away too—how about ten o'clock tomorrow morning?"
George laughed. "We'll be there," he promised, just as
happy as I was. I wakened Fern and told her and called
some other good friends I knew would be interested. I
had a smile on my face that just wouldn't come off for
the next few minutes.

But after the first elation wore off, I fell quiet,
almost subdued—suffused with a sense of profound
gratitude, almost wonder. Here I was, a man seventy-six
years old—and a man who would be seventy-seven
before this new season was finished, and yet I had just
been entrusted with bringing another year of music and
entertainment to our wonderful audience. How lucky I
was! How lucky my Musical Family and I were. We'd
rather sing and make music than eat! Well, maybe not
that, but there's nothing we'd rather do, and I thought
perhaps that was the reason I was now feeling such
tremendous, almost overpowering emotion. But, no,
there was more to it than that, something else, something I couldn't quite put my finger on. I thought about
it. Was it Don and Sam and the wonderful work they'd
been doing for me all these years? Yes, it was partly
that. Was it my feeling of great gratitude to our sponsor,
Matty Rosenhaus, for his faith in us year after year and
his own warm friendship? Yes, of course, it was that too.

But it was more. It was the realization that the
people of America liked us—maybe even loved us—and
were telling us so, once again. They had kept us on the
air for twenty-four years; now we were going into our
twenty-fifth, and they were asking us to stay—and
play—for yet another year.

I've had a lot of honors in my life. I had just
been awarded several more in the preceding few days.

And all those honors meant a great deal to me, a very great deal.

But I realized, sitting there quietly in my music room, that nothing would ever mean quite so much to me as the unstinting, loving, and loyal friendship of the people of America.

That is the highest honor of all.

Part Six

"This I Believe"

22.

This I Believe

My dear friends ... We are now nearing the end of the twentieth century. Only a couple more decades and we will move ahead into the year 2000. What a great day that will be! Maybe, if the Good Lord is willing, I'll even be around to share it—ninety-seven seems like a nice round age to live to. But even if I'm not, I will know that I have been blessed with one of the most truly happy lives any human being could live, and I am deeply, eternally grateful.

And even if I'm not here to share that great day, my hopes and dreams will go forward with this nation. I've often tried—in songs and in music, in books and in talks—to express just how I feel about this land. But I would imagine that anyone who knows the story of my life must know how I feel. Nowhere else on earth could a young farm boy, with no education and no formal musical training, be privileged to build such a wonderful Musical Family—and make friends with so many millions of people.

It is because of my great love for our country, that I feel such deep concern. It seems to me that we are at a time and in a place where we must make our choices—our options for the future. To me, the choices are clear-cut: We can either continue on the path we seem to have chosen in the past few decades—that of depending on the government for many of our needs, and accepting a range of moral standards so broad there are really no standards left. Or, we can return to the principle of accepting responsibility for our own lives, and begin living up to the strict, undeviating moral requirements of our Judeo-Christian heritage.

I guess I don't have to tell you which side I'm on! I've always been on the strict side, partly because of my upbringing and partly because it's been proven to me, over and over again during my long life, that we treasure most, the things that come hardest to us. Whatever comes too easily loses its appeal, so that a life of ease—of giving in to every urge that comes along— soon loses its charm. While a life of hard work and service to others is the one that brings lasting happiness.

So I hope—I pray—that we will choose the personal responsibility and strict moral codes which will not only enhance our own lives but the country's as well.

I hope one of our options for the future will be liberty! I hope we'll hold on to our freedom and make it stronger. Oh, how I hope for that! You and I were born into freedom—we know no other way of life; freedom is our heritage. But, we've been losing it over the past few decades little by little, allowing the government to take over more and more of the responsibilities which should rightfully be ours. As I see it, the only way to get our freedom back is to take our responsibilities back. Freedom comes high. It cannot be earned lightly. If we want it, we have to pay the price, and the price is building ourselves and our children into strong, self-reliant citizens, eager and capable of taking care of ourselves! That's the kind of people who built this country. America wasn't built by citizens who sat around waiting for the welfare check to come in. It was built by strong men and strong women who were willing to pay the price that freedom requires. I pray that we Americans will choose to pay that price—and keep our freedom.

If we save freedom we will also save our free-enterprise system, and I certainly hope we can, because it is the greatest boon to the average man that has ever come along. If you need any proof just take a look at our standard of living. Better yet, take a trip around the world, and then come back and compare. You'll realize how good we have it here. There's no country like ours. There never has been.

Free Enterprise is what gave us our wonderful life. There have been a lot of fancy definitions for it, but to me it has always meant simply "Pleasing the people." That covers all the salient points—competition in a free and open market, trying to make your product better than anyone else's, being free to compete without controls from any source. That's the essence of free enterprise, and I would be deeply grieved to see us lose it. But we *will* lose it, unless we retain the freedom it takes to keep free enterprise operating. The moment we minimize our freedom—make it smaller, put controls and limits on it—we begin to lose it and with it our way of life. It's too good to lose! Let's hold on to it. I pray we commit ourselves to that purpose.

I'd like to address myself specifically to our young folks now. You have such a special place in my heart—I have such great hopes for you! You are presently in the morning of your life, but by the year 2000 you will be adults. Whatever choices you make now will decide the kind of life you will be living then. I hope you will choose wisely, my dear young friends. If I may give you a word of advice, I would suggest that first of all, you find out what kind of work you want to do throughout your life. If you don't know—look around. Get a job in various businesses (I'm doing all I can to help you along that line!) When you find the profession or craft you like get a job in some phase of it—after school, on weekends, whenever you can. And then, make yourself the very best at whatever you choose!

And don't be afraid to make mistakes. Look on "failures" as learning experiences and be grateful for them. Every businessperson, including me, has had a long, long list of failures. I'd be happy to list mine for you, but it would take another book! I agree with George Hamid, the famous showman who built the Steel Pier in Atlantic City, who said, "Whatever success I've attained, I owe to my failures. A hungry showman learns more from one resounding failure than he does from two successes!" How true. I've often thought God sends us hard spots and troubles deliberately, to teach and instruct, to test our mettle, and to help us develop the strength of character that lies idle in us. I can truthfully say that the hardships and disappointments in my life helped me more than anything else to achieve my goals.

If I were your age now, I would not only plunge into the work of my choice, I'd try to live my life according to strict moral standards. I know it's much more difficult today than when I was young! Then, we had moral standards which everybody accepted. Not everyone lived up to them, true. But we knew what was right and what was wrong—and lived in a time when "right" was admired. It gave our lives a sense of peace and direction which is very much needed today. So I hope you will look for moral truths— "God's Laws," I call them. I hope you will accept them and live up to them, no matter how hard they are or how much your friends may tease you. You'll be happier if you do.

You young people are the hope of the world. Of course you've heard that before, but it is quite true, because America is the last stronghold of the freedom, compassion, and scientific know-how that gives hope to the rest of the world. If you succeed, so will America, and so will the rest of the free world.

I have learned, through my lifetime, that nothing builds character, nothing builds success, nothing builds personal happiness quite so much as "work." That's why I'm trying so hard to make it freely available to you, with no strings attached. That's why I'm trying, in the autumn of my life, to help people understand the pitfalls you are facing, and make the legal changes which will permit you to work with an employer who will hand on to you what he has learned, and help you step out of yourself into the broader world of your work, your profession, your America. If I could leave to you young people only the chance to work freely, at whatever you wish, with whomever you wish, at any *age* you wish ... I would feel my life had been well spent.

I hope that by the year 2000, working together, we will have eased the dominance of the institutions which now curtail our freedom and constrict our lives. I hope we will have taken the steps to free our youngsters—and our nation—from laws which now unfairly hold them back and retard their growth.

I hope we will have learned that life without freedom is unthinkable. And that freedom must be earned, every day of the year, through our own work and diligence.

Most of all, I hope we will have learned that to live a life of fulfillment, of true satisfaction and abiding joy, we must live according to God's Laws.

That is the one truth which underlies all others. It is my hope and wish for the future, that young America will go with God.

Welk Freedom System

The Welk Freedom System is based on the principles of Free Enterprise—freedom, competition, personal growth; and determination to produce the best possible product.

Freedom
We operate in complete freedom.
No one is signed to a contract.
All employment agreements are voluntary; either the employer or employee is free to terminate the relationship at any time.

We believe this kind of total freedom generates an atmosphere which brings out the best in everyone concerned.

Training and Sharing Policies

Training Policies
1. Our training period lasts for one year.
2. All training is done on-the-job, under the personal supervision of myself, or my right-hand assistants, George Cates, Jim Hobson, Jack Imel, etc., etc.
3. All trainees are paid wages set by union, state, or federal law, during their training period. They understand that when they have successfully completed their one-year training period, they will begin to share in our profits, *in addition to their regular wage.*
4. All training is done in a very positive way, through example, encouragement, and the setting of attractive goals.

5. If criticism or correction is necessary, this is given in private.
6. We keep in mind at all times, that we are training not only in job skills, but in character traits too.
7. We think of ourselves (management), as "parents" or "guardians," and our trainees as our adopted "children."

Sharing Policies
The spirit of "sharing" permeates our system, and is expressed in the following ways:

Profit-Sharing
1. We (the management) have contributed an amount equal to fifteen percent of our total, eligible payroll, to our Employee's Profit-Sharing Fund (the amount allowed us by the government). Employees contribute no money.
2. All monies in the profit-sharing fund are invested in an annuity contract guaranteed a minimum return up to 9 percent per year, for the exclusive use of our employees.
3. Each employee receives a percentage of this fund, as his share of the profits. His percentage is based on his annual salary.
4. Each employee receives his or her vested interest upon termination of employment for any reason whatsoever, including retirement, death, or disability.

Other Sharing
1. GIFTS AND BONUSES: Gifts and or bonuses are awarded throughout the year, whenever they are merited, for outstanding or specialized work, or simply for maintaining a high level of performance.
2. PROMOTIONS: Promotions within the organization

are also given whenever merited. The increased salary provides an increased share of the profits.

3. Company-owned homes and cars are available for key people for vacations, etc.
4. Voluntary contributions by management are donated to employees' medical and life-insurance programs, pension and welfare funds.
5. "Moonlighting" is allowed as a way for employees to augment their incomes, the only restriction being that their work with us comes first.
6. "FAMILY" SHARING: This is the heart of our entire concept, the most important aspect of our entire sharing program. We function as a "family," taking pride in each other's accomplishments, as well as in our own. This results in tremendous achievements, not only on an individual basis, but for the organization as a whole.

   We create and maintain this "family" feeling by exhibiting a continuing and genuine interest in our people—at the studio, in our office, and occasionally at my home, discussing their futures and trying always to do what's best for *them*.

   Every business has its own requirements, and each employer will create a family feeling in his own way. For me, it springs quite naturally from my conviction that ours is a "family" business, and everyone in it is a member of our family. In my mind they are my children; and I try to do for them what I would do if they were my own.

Finally, we rely on God's Laws to guide us in all our endeavors, and deepen the bonds of affection among and between us.

"This I Believe"

The Lawrence Welk Credo

I BELIEVE...

1. We learn and develop ourselves better by "doing" than any other way. For this reason, we should allow and encourage all people—especially young people—to work at any age they wish.

2. America needs a voluntary apprentice program, and the younger you start, the better your chances of developing your potential.

3. We have harmed our young people by making it so difficult for them to work and develop their talents for the future. Therefore, I believe we should repeal the child labor law.

4. A businessman can help his business by sharing his profits with those who help him earn them.

5. People develop best in freedom. No contracts, no legal ties, just complete freedom. Knowing you can leave, often makes you want to stay.

6. Allowing your employees to "moonlight" on other jobs, often returns them to you as an improved version of themselves.

7. "Caring" for your fellow-workers creates a family closeness that not only produces a superior relationship, but a superior product.

8. It is in giving that we receive. "Give, and it shall be given unto you," is a law of life that works—mentally, morally, socially, and economically.

9. A nation without morals is a nation headed for trouble. Our Constitution, and the laws of God made this the greatest country in the world. I believe we must return to them, if we wish to save our nation as we have known it.

10. One of the great laws of life is this: Do good to everyone and harm to no one.